Realities and Visions

REALITIES AND VISIONS
The Church's Mission Today

edited by FURMAN C. STOUGH
URBAN T. HOLMES, III

with a Foreword by John Maury Allin

A CROSSROAD BOOK
THE SEABURY PRESS • NEW YORK

The Seabury Press
815 Second Avenue
New York, N.Y. 10017

Copyright ©1976 by The Seabury Press, Inc.

All rights reserved. No part of this book may be reproduced,
stored in a retrieval system, or transmitted, in any form or
by any means, electronic, mechanical, photocopying, recording,
or otherwise, without the written permission of The Seabury Press.

Printed in the United States of America

LIBRARY OF CONGRESS CATALOGING IN PUBLICATION DATA
Main entry under title:
Realities and visions.
"A Crossroad book."
Bibliography: p.
1. Protestant Episcopal Church in the U.S.A.—Doctrinal and
controversial works—Addresses, essays, lectures.   2. Mission of
the church—Addresses, essays, lectures.   I. Stough, Furman C.,
1928-   II. Holmes, Urban Tigner, 1930-
BX5935.R4   260   76-21086
ISBN 0-8164-2130-7

contents

FOREWORD — vii
  John Maury Allin
PREFACE — ix
  Furman C. Stough and
  Urban T. Holmes, III

I. National and World Missions
  1. Five Original Goals — 3
     George D. Browne
  2. Our World Mission — 8
     Edmond L. Browning
  3. The Church is Small Communities — 16
     Roger J. White
  4. Ecumenism and the Consultation
     on Church Union — 23
     John M. Krumm
  5. Anglican and Roman Catholic — 30
     Jean Henkel Johnson
  6. Stewardship: The Mission of Giving — 42
     Furman C. Stough

II. Renewal, Evangelism, Education for Ministry
  7. Contemporary Spirituality:
     Some Structures and Styles — 51
     Dolores R. Leckey
  8. Evangelism in the Church: An Overview — 60
     O. C. Edwards, Jr.
  9. The Future for Evangelism — 77
     Louis J. Willie
  10. Church Education for Tomorrow — 84
      John H. Westerhoff III
  11. Fulfilling the Body of Christ — 92
      Philip Deemer
  12. The Ministry of the Laity:
      A Ten-Year Project — 99
      Arthur E. Zannoni

13. What is our Mission to Youth Today?   106
    John W. Yates II
14. The Tragic Continuum as a
    Basis for Pastoral Theology   113
    William C. Spong
15. Religious Orders: The Order of
    St. Benedict   122
    Anthony Damron, O.S.B.
16. Theological Education in the
    Next Decade   125
    Charles L. Winters

III. *The Church in Society*

17. An American Indian Viewpoint   137
    Marllene Campbell
18. The Role of the Urban Church:
    Its Problems and Opportunities   144
    Paul Moore, Jr.
19. The Church and Hunger:
    The On-Going Challenge   150
    Norman J. Faramelli
20. Medicine: Some Questions
    about its Future   158
    Clifton K. Meador, M.D.
21. Current Ethical Issues: An Overview   169
    James M. Childress
22. Once Again: To Comfort or
    to Challenge?   177
    Urban T. Holmes III

CONTRIBUTORS   185

BIBLIOGRAPHY   187

foreword

In 1973 efforts were initiated to address the pressing matters of priesthood and sexuality in the Church. The plan that emerged was to publish two books in which various perspectives would receive attention and consideration. As work progressed on *To Be A Priest* and *Male and Female*, it became increasingly clear to me that a third and missing part of these written mosaics about Christianity in our time was a consideration of the Church and its mission. *Realities and Visions*, the third and final volume in the series, is an effort to speak to that missing dimension by surveying the principal questions and topics facing the Church today.

In each instance I have asked the contributors to write about some visions they have for the Church in the next ten years, and to discuss these in relation to the realities they perceive in our life together. The three sections of the book represent the basic parts of our ministry today: National and World Missions; Renewal, Evangelism, and Education for Ministry; and the Church in Society.

Inevitably, one might have added more to these considerations, for the topic of the Church's mission today is such an immense one. However, the assignment to the contributors was to offer some visions so that our perceptions and goals, and our hopes for the Church, might be enriched and replenished. I earnestly hope we might have those kinds of visions and encouragement to press on in our ministry.

Now, as so often in its history, the Church is confronted with a multitude of opportunities and problems, with competing voices and directions, with almost overpowering temptations of spirit and matter. Visions and dreams pressed against these realities may aid us in seeking to be faithful to our calling as servants of Jesus Christ. It is that high calling that challenges us and calls us on to each new hour and day. I hope our visions can meet that challenge, and I pray that this Church can bear faithful witness to that wondrous treasure which has been given by our blessed Lord.

John Maury Allin
Presiding Bishop
The Episcopal Church

preface

This is the third volume in a series of three mosaics which the Presiding Bishop initiated in preparation for the 1976 General Convention. The first two volumes arose out of the ongoing conversation within the Church in regard to the priesthood and sexuality. Therefore, they possessed a particular focus on which theology and the human sciences were brought to bear. This volume seeks, not to speak to "issues," but to provide an opportunity for a spectrum of churchpeople to discuss the ministry and mission of the Church.

We asked our contributors to take the title of the book seriously—*Realities and Visions*. We did not want them to dwell on the problems of the Church, but to be cognizant of the place of the Church, just as it is, as we enter the last quarter of the twentieth century. We also wanted them to look to the next ten years and to describe, as hopefully as they could, the direction they would like the Church to move in.

As the reader will note, the authors of these essays come from all areas of the Church's life. We have carefully sought to gather young and old, male and female, black, white, and red, evangelical and Catholic, professional and amateur. The result is a rather mixed bag. Yet, as we see it, it is a very interesting collection; one which calls our attention to some particular concerns that are often overlooked in favor of other debates now monopolizing the Church.

First, there is a clear affirmation of faith in these essays. Ten years ago many people were predicting the demise of the institutional Church, if not of organized religion itself. Whether or not it be the work of John Yates, the reflection of Louis Willie, the insights of Clifton Meador, or the affirmation of John Krumm, there is an expectation that God is working in his Church in this world, which pervades everything that is written here.

Second, there is a clear sense of priorities. These are the words of people who want to get on with the business of the Church and have some ideas of how that might be done. There is no talk here of schism in the face of the possible ordination of women to the priesthood or of despair over prayerbook revision. There is a clear feeling that Christians ought to know what they believe and witness to it. This does not mean that there is a total agreement as to what that belief is; rather, there is a rich diversity of interest. For example, contrast the articles of Roger White and Paul

Moore, Norman Faramelli and Marllene Campbell, Jean Johnson and George Browne.

Third, some articles are full of detailed statements of what the Church ought to be doing and others are groping. Delores Leckey, for example, runs through a whole series of things which are happening because of this renewed interest in the life of the Spirit in the Church. O. C. Edwards clearly spells out eleven points which he thinks are the particular attractions of Anglicanism today. John Westerhoff has a unique and clear vision of where Christian education ought to go, as does Charles Winters for theological education. Philip Deemer and William Spong are more discursive, providing the reader with an opportunity to fill out his own agenda in the light of their reflections upon the life of the Church.

Fourth, we do not see the widely touted opposition between spiritual interest and concern for the world in these essays. This is extremely heartening. Obviously the authors, whether explicitly or abstractly, take the Incarnation with full seriousness, believing that God is both transcendent and immanent. If we are to live the life of the Spirit, we must also manifest the fruits of that Spirit in our commitment to the Church through our stewardship and in our service to our fellow man, both within the community and without. Arthur Zannoni's and James Childress' essays clearly speak to that, as well as our own offerings.

It is our intention that these articles will serve to give hope to those for whom the current debates within the Church have proved to be disillusioning. It is certainly our desire that we can supply a vision—albeit one of many parts, not neatly fitted together—which will charge the imagination of our readers. It is our belief that we live in a most religious age; one in which we need only be open to the presence of God in our daily lives and be willing to share our deepest aspirations for one another in order to be able to see the opportunities that lie before us. The material in this book is for reflection and careful pondering. It reflects a cross-section of thoughtful churchpeople, calling us to work together. We hope that the reader will accept the differences, both within the text and between himself and the authors, and find in the disagreements, the incongruities, and the incompleteness of these essays room for him to move in and join the holy quest upon which we are all invited.

Furman C. Stough
Urban T. Holmes

PART I
National and World Missions

chapter 1

FIVE ORIGINAL GOALS

George D. Browne

In 1836, when the Domestic & Foreign Missionary Society of the Protestant Episcopal Church, U.S.A. (PECUSA) sent its very first missionary to a foreign land, the Foreign Committee of that society gave instructions which set some policy guidelines for PECUSA's overseas work. These I would like to review briefly. That first missionary was the Rev. Dr. Thomas S. Savage, M.D., from the Diocese of Connecticut, and his destination was Liberia, West Africa. Those instructions are found in the *Spirit of Missions*, Vol. 1, 1836, pp. 339–342.
Excerpts of them read like this:

The great aim of your Mission is towards the native Africans. You are sent to establish a mission which seeks nothing less than the christianizing of Africa; and although it is but a small portion which may be attained by your Mission, yet we must never lose sight of the end.

It will become you, then, to take every opportunity of inquiring into the condition of the native nations around you, in the interior, and on the leeward coast; to ascertain their character, the nature and course of their trade, the spirit they manifest towards the teachers of true religion, and, in short, whatever of authentic information, that may serve to inform the Church of the actual position of the native population. (The Africans are travelling people, and, without trusting to a single source, you may gather from those among whom you will mingle with valuable information.)

In making personal excursions into the country, while you aim not at becoming a mere traveller, you may still to some extent, become an exploring Missionary.

The Committee wish you to inquire as to the propriety of hereafter establishing Missions on the leeward coast, those marts for inland trade; and also of penetrating to the nation of the Ashantees of Dahomey, and others, in that region of Western Africa.

You will pay attention to the language of the native nations, and their dialects, with a view of their gradual reduction to a written tongue.

The Committee feel that in the exercise of your knowledge as a physician, you will not be slow to answer the calls of humanity. They prefer, however, that you should not act as recognised physician of the colony, lest such a responsibility should too much increase your cares, and detach you from the Mission. Bear in mind that you have now taken upon you to be *a faithful dispenser of the word of God, and of his holy sacraments*. You are to make this a primary object, and your medical services must be subordinate, or rather auxiliary to it.

You are to seek distinctly, to form a visible Church of Christ, gathering (as the Lord shall prosper you, and give power to his work) "a congregation of faithful men," under the ordinance of that Church, which we believe to be formed upon the apostles and prophets, Jesus Christ himself being the chief corner-stone. In this work you will be steadily encouraged by the evident blessing which has attended the forms of our worship, among the most ignorant nations; the growing testimony to this will strengthen your faith.

I take the liberty to paraphrase these instructions. "Never lose sight" that PECUSA is in a foreign country for the purpose of evangelization. In doing so, it must seek to discover from the area and culture what can be used to communicate the Gospel and evoke the appropriate response from the people. It is to encourage the missionary jurisdictions to be mission-minded and "penetrate" neighboring countries as partners in mission. If the Church is to affect the lives of the people to whom it ministers, we are to "pay attention to the language of the native nations, and their dialects" with the view of translating the liturgy and the Bible, and enabling them to express their understanding and love for God in creative and indigenous concepts.

Ordained missionaries are to be faithful dispensers of the Word and the sacraments. All other skills and services are to be subordinate and auxiliary to this work. This role must issue forth in a worshipping community, a congregation of the faithful. Not included in the above extract, but in the original instructions is the warning, "do not entertain extravagant expectations as to the result of your Mission," but, "seeking to be steadily faithful . . . aspire to be a faithful follower of Him . . . who can labor that others might enter His labor."

Although Dr. Savage was sent to Africa 140 years ago, the instructions and policy guidelines given to him are applicable to our situation today, and will be so for a long time. From this summary I would like to make five points:

Five Original Goals 5

    1. The selection process for appointing missionaries should be reviewed.

    2. We must seek to permeate the customs and traditions of our people with the Gospel.

    3. Overseas jurisdictions should be encouraged to be mission-minded.

    4. Closer attention should be given to the local languages.

    5. Establish "worshipping communities" with indigenous structures and forms that can be supported locally.

The call to Mission has equal and eternal claims on all Christian bodies. PECUSA should continue more than ever to do mission wherever it is needed. The aim of the Church, as stated in 1836, is to evangelize. Interpreted in current overseas concepts, it does not end with baptism and confirmation. The individual must be followed up until his everyday life gives evidence that he has had a personal encounter with the living Lord, and that the fruits of his life indicate that Christ is his Lord.

This task suggests that we review our screening and selection process for the appointment of missionaries overseas. The importance of personal witness cannot be overstated. Past experience, the new developments taking place in overseas dioceses, and the unique place of the United States in world politics, dictate that PECUSA missionary personnel for overseas should be selected on the basis of criteria other than the ones currently being used: request from overseas, needs, and talents. It is time to give other criteria, including personal witness and the guidance of the Holy Spirit, in the selection process.

The missionary is required to work among the natives. To do so effectively, he is to study their customs and traditions, not at an orientation program in New York but while in the field. This is crucial, not only for information but as an indispensable asset in his work. If Christianity is to affect the whole man so that his everyday life shows evidence of personal encounter with the living Christ, it must first infiltrate his customs and traditions. It must "discover" what is available and valuable in the given culture and area, with the view of eventually making Christ enculturated. We missionaries are to seek "points of contact" which the Holy Spirit can use to affect positive Christian changes in the customs and traditional practices.

It is important to bear in mind at the outset, that the foreign missionaries are "sent"; and will later be withdrawn from the mission field. But the Church, once established, is timeless. The natives of a given missionary area are *permanent factors in the Church.* They cannot be withdrawn. Therefore, at the outset, efforts should be made for the Christian Gospel to speak to those factors which dynamically undergird and actively support the soul-center of their relationships. At this moment in our history, overseas jurisdictions cannot establish the needed spiritual, moral, and financial base for sustained support everywhere, but only within their indigenous resources. In our search for an indigenous expression of Christianity based on our encounter with Christ in our culture, we might develop a new form of Christianity, different from that of the West. But there is place for pluralistic forms in the New Testament.

It is not enough to invest our traditions with the Christian Gospel. Evangelism includes sharing with one another what Jesus means to you, and seeking response and/or commitment. The former is "telling"; the latter is "doing." One is evangelism; the other is ministry, and they complement one another. Hence the Foreign Committee instructed Dr. Savage that his mission "should go beyond the boundary" of the country in which it began. It must be "Partners in the Mission" of God, taking responsibility for both evangelism and ministry. It is clear from the instructions that evangelism takes preference. Though the missionaries to Africa established schools and hospitals and organized other community services, Dr. Savage was requested to subordinate all skills and services to the Word and the sacraments.

Present-day missionary strategy needs to emphasize that God's mission of "telling" and "doing" has equal claims on all of his children; and consequently, all PECUSA overseas jurisdictions should be encouraged to take on mission projects outside their geographical boundaries. This is deeply rooted in the divine commission and buttressed by spiritual freedom. It should be a high priority. It gives the overseas churches a sense of mission and builds up a spirit of mutual responsibility and interdependence in the body of Christ. It provides a climate for us as a body of Christ to reorient our missionary approach.

"Overseas churches" is a term that has been traditionally used to mean the missionary work outside the continents of the United States and Europe, and which was begun and sponsored by Europeans and Americans. The reorientation to which I refer, and which is fostered by mission-minded Churches, will also help the "overseas churches" to see that Europe and America are also "overseas," and that it is incumbent on us all to "tell" them the good news of what God has done for us spiritually, as well as to "do" something for them under the divine commission. It will bring out the truism that no one people is the sole custodian of the revelation of God or has the sole responsibility for mission of God's Church.

While it is true that the principle of "Partners in Mission" and "telling" the good news of the Gospel does not require a great deal of literacy, it is of extreme importance that the "teller" understands his story and is able to communicate his experience. The Church cannot take roots among a people, unless it speaks their language.

Western theological thought cannot be transposed into a non-Western situation. Attempts to do this have done harm to the Church's effectiveness overseas. For overseas jurisdictions, the contents of theological instructions has been foreign; and the joy of theological reflection minimal. Theological education has been taught by a foreign faculty in a European language. The emphasis upon academic performance is at the expense of a shared ministry. This experience makes the Foreign Committee's instruction, that "you pay attention to the language of the native nations," a timely guideline for us as we map our work for the future.

The establishing of a worshiping community of the faithful is one of the ultimate goals. I see all services to a given people and community within the framework of this "visible Church of Christ." In this pursuit, it is only helpful to say that expatriate missionaries should "hang loose," be open-minded, and let growth take place from within the local church, so that authentic native structures and forms emerge that can be supported locally. This holds true even for new mission areas established by missionary jurisdictions. In the past, missionary societies have supported structures. We should be careful how we impose structures on people. When the missionary personnel withdrew, the funds used to support the structures are also withdrawn. Hence, we must plan and develop structures that do not alienate people and can be supported locally.

The final note of warning. Do not entertain extravagant expectations of gathering the fruits of your labor now, but leave that "evidence of success" wholly to God. For we are called to be steadily faithful in missions—not successful.

In summary, as we envision world mission in the mid-seventies and eighties, we will do well to find out what our forefathers had in mind when they organized the missionary arm of this Church. Their policies are as tenable today as they were at that time. For we can see the future clearer if we stand on the shoulders of the past.

chapter 2

OUR WORLD MISSION

Edmond L. Browning

The Presiding Bishop wrote to me that in order to assist the people of this Church to come to grips with some of the current questions related to our common tasks, a number of us were being asked to write about the Church's mission in the world. I was asked to say where I would like to see the Church go in the next ten years, with particular emphasis on world mission in the context of the Episcopal Church's work overseas. What you are about to read is my understanding of the direction in which the Church is going today, as well as my vision for its future life. My hope is that the reader will find this essay not only informative but, even more, an inspiring vision to share with others.

The key to understanding the Church's mission is being sensitive to where God is at work in his creation, where he is calling us today to join him, and where he will be calling us through the next ten years. In 1959, together with my family, I went to Okinawa to join the Church's missionary work there. Out of this experience of twelve years came a learning that I believe has importance for the understanding of mission.

We went to Okinawa for many reasons—some good and some not so good. Certainly one of those reasons was to be in some way a means by which God in Christ could be introduced to the Okinawans. The understanding that I would like to share with you—that I believe is a key to understanding mission—is one that I learned gradually as I came to know the Okinawan people. Their lives were lived in beautiful simplicity, always with a deep caring and concern. You could see this in the way they emphasized the family, for they saw it as the cornerstone of society. You could sense it in the way they related to children and the aged. You could feel it as you watched them struggle for justice and dignity when they were being tossed to and fro politically. You knew it in the way they related themselves to nature and in their appreciation of their environment.

I came to understand that I was not there to introduce God to the Okinawans or the Okinawans to God. I came to realize that he was there before I arrived—before any missionary reached those shores—and that I was there because he had called me to join him in one of the places in which he was already at work. Again, the key to understanding the Church's mission is to seek to discern in this confused, suffering, and starving world where God is at work and how we might join him.

If we begin with this basic assumption—that God is at work within his creation seeking to free, to enable, to bring man to himself; that it is he who initiates this mission; that it is he who sets these concerns in our hearts and calls us to join him in these tasks—then, I think we can give thanks that the Episcopal Church has in the past few years responded in some significant ways to joining God in his mission.

In the sixties, under the dynamic leadership of John Hines, we were led to rethink the meaning of mission, to see God's call to reach out to the oppressed and the victims of racism and injustice. The seventies began with an apparent change in direction as the spiritual renewal of the Church seemed to be the call responded to by many. Along with the emphasis on spiritual renewal came a reawakening of the essential place of evangelism within the mission of the Church. In the fall of 1974 Bishop John Allin called this Church to acknowledge the hunger crisis that exists domestically as well as world-wide. He called us to acknowledge that we were a part of the problem as well as of the solution.

To what degree this can be said to be true, I'm not certain, but I think we can say that within the last decade there has been a valuable learning experienced at most levels within the life of the Church. That learning is that the mission of the Church is never an either/or proposition. It is never either social action or spiritual renewal, but both. It is never either primary evangelism or a struggle for global justice, but both. It is never either feeding the hungry or human and material development, but both. Mission is as varied as God would have it. Mission is of God, and as it is he who calls us and sets the priorities. His mission is never static. There are times in history when he demands and calls more in one direction than another, and in obedience to the oneness in mission, it behooves us both individually and corporately to be sensitive to one another as God makes his mission known to us through the lives of others.

Dr. José Miguez-Bonino, Dean of Graduate Studies at the Higher Institute of Theological Studies in Buenos Aires, has written:

The worst danger for mission at this time is reductionism. In reductionism we try to tie God down to one form of work—personal or social, institutional or spontaneous, intellectual or practical. God's strategy is aways many-sided and unpredictable. He defines for us the direction in which he is moving and invites us to follow him. But he goes as he wills and refuses to give us job descriptions valid for all. He defines the job in the situation. What he demands is availability and obedience.

Dr. Miguez-Bonino expresses a growing consensus that the mission is *one* for the Church, wherever it may be; that the mission of the Church is *one* in that it comes from the one triune God and his hopes and intentions for the reconciliation of all men. His call to the Church is *one*, even though the gifts he shares with the Church, and the given responses of particular Churches in particular situations to this call, are manifold.

I have tried to affirm the responses to mission in which the Episcopal Church has engaged itself in the past few years out of a particular theological base; at the same time I have tried to set the framework in which we can see God's call within the next ten years. To summarize: God is at work in his creation, calling his people to join him in the mission he identifies as being imperative for the day. Our obedience comes in our response and commitment to the oneness in mission in all its diversified challenges.

To relate this to the "American Episcopal Church's work overseas," I would like to recall an extremely important recognition made by the Anglican Congress in 1963 in the document "Mutual Responsibility and Interdependence" (MRI), a document that has deeply influenced the mission strategy of the Anglican Communion. This recognition is beautifully phrased in the 1973 Dublin report of the second meeting of the Anglican Consultative Council: "There is but one mission and this one mission is shared by the world-wide Christian community. The responsibility for mission in any place belongs primarily to the Church in that place. However, the universality of the Gospel and the oneness of God's mission means also that this mission must be shared in each and every place with fellow Christians from each and every part of the world with their distinctive insights and contributions."

This emphasis and recognition of the Church having been planted in all corners of the globe, with the primary responsibility for the mission in that place belonging to that Church, challenged our previous concept of mission being the movement of the developed Christian society to the underdeveloped non-Christian societies. It further challenged our practices of control and dominant leadership patterns, and questioned the place and role of the missionary. And finally, it challenged the entire Anglican Church to see that we are all interdependent within the body of Christ, all having both much to receive from others as well as much to give. The American Church, however, still has a difficult time appreciating this fact in any deep sense. There are many ways I think one could identify how this basic recognition has influenced the mission strategy of our Church, and I would like to identify the three which I believe must be given the most serious consideration within the next ten years.

First, it seems to me that the recognition that the Church is planted in all corners of the globe requires us to be concerned for people and their problems rather than geographical areas. In the past the mission of the Church was concerned with people. However, the emphasis I would like to make is the Church's mission to the whole range of human problems in testimony to the saving concern of God. This leads me to say that in our overseas relationships we should be concerned about how we as a Church might help ourselves, as well as the people and the Church in that place, to face and deal with the issues of poverty, hunger, population, justice, and human rights. The Rev. Dr. T. K. Jones, Jr. has written:

An authentic task of mission today concerns the ways by which men and women can free themselves from oppressive systems that keep them poor, illiterate, subjugated, and thwarted in their efforts to achieve for themselves the quality of life possible for them in their society.

Last summer I spent several days in the Diocese of El Salvador, the smallest diocese in the Anglican Communion and yet one with a tremendous sense of mission to the people of that nation. Several years ago the Rev. Luis Serrano began a program named "CREDHO," which is designed to enable the poor to come to know in various ways a quality of life that had not been known to them previously. I saw a community health program, not being imposed from the outside but being designed and managed by the people themselves. I witnessed classes and field experimentation in agricultural training designed to give the most production in any given area. One afternoon I went with Father Serrano and Dr. Rosa Cesnares, a lawyer, to watch them assist some 250 *campesinos* (farmers) form an association to defend their small pieces of land against a large landowner.

For four days I watched a priest, a lawyer, a doctor, a young Peace Corps worker, and a community of the faithful exercising a ministry, not *to* the poor but *with* the poor. It is a ministry which has heard God speaking out of the poverty and injustices being experienced by a part of his creation. It is a ministry that, having forced on it conditions of poverty, hunger, and social injustice, has sought to respond faithfully in helping to change these conditions by enabling the poor themselves to act.

The American Episcopal Church, whether at the national, diocesan, or parish level, should have within all its missionary strategies for overseas relationships a basic commitment to the liberation and humanizing of mankind. El Salvador is but one diocese among many that seeks to deal with the full range of human problems that restrict the dignity of the individual. I think that it is significant that the Presiding Bishop's Fund for World Relief sees as one of its primary tasks the participation in the support of development programs which are going to enable people to deal creatively and productively with their problems. Likewise, the United Thank Offering in its granting process recognizes that training for human development in all its aspects is essential to working for global justice. A concluding thought: it is my conviction that this Church is being called by Christ himself to use our leadership and our human and financial resources in every conceivable way to enter into this range of problems—into the lives of the poor and the oppressed.

Moving now to another concern, the Anglican Congress and its document of "Mutual Responsibility and Interdependence" challenged seriously the American Episcopal Church's relations with its overseas jurisdictions. The concept of interdependence challenged both the dependent role of the jurisdictions on the national structure as well as the paternalistic stance of the National Church toward these jurisdictions. The National Church has had to face the question of whether it was seeking to *enable* these jurisdictions in their process of developing a mature life, or was it indeed, through various ways, treating them as adolescents—or even worse acting as a parent not willing to trust or to let go. We had to reexamine the purpose of these ministries: Were they really to be indigenous churches with indigenous leadership related to and part of the very culture in which they lived or were they to be a mere reflection of the American tradition?

Over the past thirteen years, these questions have been and are continuing to be asked as policy decisions are being made regarding the mission strategy of the Episcopal Church in relationship to these jurisdictions. A great deal of credit has to be given to the Overseas Review Committee, to the Joint Commission on World Mission, and to a great many dedicated people for the significant changes that have been made in relationship to the belief that "self-government, self-support, and self-propagation are the marks of an independent, mature Church." Just to name a few of the changes: overseas dioceses may now elect their own bishop rather than having it done in the House of Bishops; all property of a given diocese once held by the National Church has been transferred to that diocese; overseas bishops in consultation with one another decide about their budgets, instead of the national office distributing what is available. Through their coalition, the overseas bishops themselves, as well as the national leadership, have learned the meaning of interdependence in a variety of ways.

Through all these changes the jurisdictions are experiencing a new identity—a national identity that gives their smaller family a sense of particular purpose within their own country. There is a growing desire among most to seek an autonomy for their Church which will make them less dependent upon the Church in the United States. In actuality, some of the dioceses wish to leave the American structure, not to be "independent" from us but so that the meaning of interdependence within the body of Christ might have more significance when they can meet with us as equal partners rather than as the child coming to the parent. This is not new; the Province of Brazil was formed from dioceses which were once a part of the American Church. The Diocese of Okinawa, now the eleventh diocese of the Japanese Episcopal Church, was once a part of our General Convention. At the 1976 General Convention, the Diocese of Liberia is petitioning to become an associated diocese of the Province of West Africa. The Diocese of Costa Rica is planning a similar step in September. Other overseas dioceses, although not as far along as those mentioned above, are doing similar planning.

It is essential to consider, in terms of what is hoped for in the next ten years, one of the reasons that other overseas dioceses have not moved as fast toward autonomy. These jurisdictions, for the most part, have achieved a real measure of self-government and self-propagation, but self-support is still beyond their reach. The overseas bishops and their dioceses find themselves in a real dilemma about this problem. The goal of self-support means not having to ask for increased budget support to retain the status quo. The need to ask for support, in fact, only increases their dependency.

The overseas dioceses are taking several approaches to this problem—re-evaluation of programs, increased local stewardship, initiation of new forms of ministries, changes in institutional life-styles. Most important of all, they are seeking capital funding to provide investments for their jurisdictions that will supplement the process of each diocese moving toward autonomy. With the assistance of the United Thank Offering, an Overseas Development Fund was established to meet this critical need for capital funding. It is sincerely hoped that the General Convention will share their vision and give this fund a visibility that will call every member of this Church to the task of assisting the overseas jurisdictions in their respective mission and ministry.

I would affirm that much good has happened during the ten years following the 1963 Anglican Congress regarding the mission strategy of the Church. In these closing paragraphs I would like to state my belief that even more will happen during the second ten-year period. As Jeannie Willis has so aptly stated, the "MRI-Phase II" program began with the presentation of the Partners-in-Mission Consultation process developed at the second meeting of the Anglican Consultative Council meeting in Dublin in 1973. Very briefly, this program calls for each Province or Council within the Anglican Communion to host a consultation to which they invite other parts of the communion to join them as partners in their mission. The ingredients of such a consultation are several fold. The host province (dioceses within the province), after a good deal of preparation for the consultation, are asked to state their mission goals both as individual dioceses and also, corporately, as a province. The partners are then invited to share something of themselves with their host province, and to question, challenge, and affirm the host province as to their goals. And finally, they determine how, collectively and as partners, they can actually support the mission as determined by the host province.

We as the American Church will have participated as partners in fourteen consultations by the end of this year. There is so much that can be said for this program, so much that makes this process essential to our total mission strategy, that I would like to identify just a few of the results. First, our participation in these consultations gives to our Church a much broader picture of the mission possibilities—and our responsibilities to those possibilities within the total Anglican family—than has been previously shared. Secondly, the sharing of resources and the joint cooperation of missionary agencies to support defined efforts and projects throughout the world wide family may be as important as any development within the process. Thirdly, in the consultation itself, dioceses within the same process make some remarkable discoveries about each other, resulting in joint planning and sharing of resources that before the consultation were kept very parochial. Fourthly, the consultative process allows both the host and the partners to be able to give and to receive with integrity.

In his paper "Biblical Basis for Stewardship," R. M. Cooper writes that "one task of Christian Stewardship is to multiply the capacity for receiving—giving can be a vehicle for pride and supposed self-sufficiency; the giver is too easy a controller [of others]." The consultation process enables the invited partner to see very quickly that he is in relationship with a mature Church, filled with great vitality and having gifts that could strengthen his own Church. And yet, in the same instance, the partner's need to share and respond to the "universality of the Gospel and the oneness of God's mission" is met as the host identifies the mission challenges in his area.

It follows, therefore, that I look forward with great anticipation to the event that will provide this kind of experience of mission to the American Church. I refer to our Partners in Mission Consultation, to be held in April of 1977, to which are invited representatives of our Anglican Partner Churches.

Based on the results of such consultations in and with other Anglican Churches, it is not too much to hope that in our consultation we shall examine the meaning of mission for ourselves in new depth and wholeness.

It could be a meaningful experience for us to learn how our partners see us as we seek to do mission. The consultation offers also the potential for developing a sharing process between our dioceses as they discover common goals and heretofore unperceived resources, which in turn can strengthen our provinces and enable them for mission. We shall discover resources available to us from our partner Churches, giving us the opportunity to experience what it means to receive. We shall, by acknowledging our overall goals interdependently, be able to unify this Church in its one mission.

In summary, the "missionary era" is not a thing of the past, as some would have it. It is my vision that we are embarking on a new era of mission more exciting and more fulfilling than any we have ever known.

# chapter 3

THE CHURCH IN SMALL COMMUNITIES

Roger J. White

The rapid and wide expansion of the Church in the early centuries was due in the first place mainly to the spontaneous activity of individuals . . . a natural instinct to share with others a new-found joy . . . the early Church recognized this natural instinct and this Divine Grace and gave free scope to it.

Our present missions are not the natural homes of spontaneous expansion.

What is necessary is faith. What is needed is the kind of faith which, uniting a man to Christ, sets him on fire. Such a man can believe that others finding Christ will be set on fire also.

—Roland Allen[1]

  The works of Roland Allen are still little known, and although he wrote his books some sixty years ago, they are full of relevancy for the Church today. Allen addressed himself to the Anglican predicament during his lifetime, with its overseas missions and vast organization, but his writings also speak to our mission as a Church today. He has much to say to the Church in small communities, whether these communities are rural or urban. This article relies heavily on some of Allen's insights into the mission and ministry of the Church.
  We have tended to think more about the Church in small rural communities and ignore the vast area of small communities which are decidedly urban. An attempt will be made in this article to look at the Church in small communities generally and, while recognizing many differences be-

The Church is Small Communities 17

tween a rural and urban setting, many common problems remain because the Episcopal Church tends to be a small Christian community ministering in many small communities, both urban or rural.

In its missionary endeavors in small communities, the Church has tended to work the wrong way around. This has led to an unhealthy situation, where we find a diocese now ministering more to the needs of a church in a small community (what we call a "mission"), rather than the Church as the body of Christ, ministering to and reaching out to the community where it finds itself. Roland Allen points to this danger.

> An elaborate material machinery for the propagation of ideas seems to most of those to whom we go almost absurd. You do not want buildings and machinery to propagate ideas or a faith, you want ideas and a faith. Organization and buildings ought to follow and spring out of the working of ideas and the faith. Our organization seems to them to put the wrong things first.

We have to ask: "Are we a viable Church at all in small communities if we no longer minister but just exist to be ministered to by the rest of the Church?" We have a vocation to mission and therefore to ministry. When we live only for ourselves, we die, and we lose our objective as the people of God in our community. Perhaps change can begin most easily at the point when people sense a problem or feel a high degree of urgency; and in many churches with fewer than 150 communicants that urgency and problem often seems to be a financial one. The small local church finds itself more and more in financial difficulties supporting property and fulltime clergy. Many churches have been to a large extent "English chaplaincies" with no sense or hope of mission or ministry to the community outside themselves. Allen makes the observation which is not without its truth for today: "A mission station is indeed a contradiction in terms; mission implies movement, station implies stopping." For many of our churches we have stopped, and we do not know how to move within our present structures.

If we look at diocesan budgets for mission work, we find great amounts of diocesan energies and monies, complemented by local energy and monies, devoted to property upkeep and personnel replacement and compensation. The majority of these talents and energies are concentrated on maintaining the status quo, ministering to the people of God and to their clergy. Very little attention or energy is given to the call of the Church to preach to all people in the world and bring them to a love and knowledge of our Lord.

It becomes apparent that the Church has become indifferent to its mission and has become a dependent *only*, rather than being a dependent in order to go out and minister to the world. How we minister will reflect how effective our mission is to the community we live in. And if we are to have a mission, we must be willing to minister as a whole people of God and we will need to know how to do that.

We see many movements and their resulting organizations within the Church devoted to planning and executing attempts to pursue the mission of the Church. Much energy and money is expended in organizing and reorganizing, little on preparing the people of God, lay or clerical, to do the work in the expansion of the Church.

Expansion of the Christian faith is in essence spontaneous. Our planning, organization, and establishment of the local church has tended to freeze spontaneous expansion and to bring about self-satisfaction and apathy. Roland Allen speaks well to this point.

> In the beginning the Church was a missionary society, it added to its members mainly by the life and speech of its members, attracting to it those who were outside. Where they went, churches were organized, where they settled, men who had never heard of the Church saw the Church, and being attracted by the life, or by the speech, of its members, learned its secret, joined it, and were welcomed into it. Today members of the Church are scattered all over the world, but they do not carry the Church with them in their own persons, they very often do not desire the conversion of those among whom they live, they do not welcome them into the Church.

The spontaneity of our mission is frozen, which leads to feeble and inadequate attempts by the Church to be the people of God in the world. This unfortunately is the reality with which the Church finds itself faced today. Many attempts at reorganizing or reshuffling the same cards has not resulted in a renewal of mission for the Church in small communities or in any community. What then do we find by way of vision in the Church today?

We have been blessed in recent years with several visionaries. Such visionaries have implemented experimental ministries and approaches to mission which have in a small way initiated the defrosting of the frozen army of God's people. We have, in the years ahead, both the opportunity and the obligation to implement more fully some present-day thinking and to attempt to open up the mission work of the Church. We need to identify the bonds which hold us back and throw them loose, to find again the freedom of spontaneous expansion through the life and witness of all the members of Christ's Body. The visionaries of today have sensed the problem and feel a high degree of urgency; and now they are encouraging the Church to move.

The rethinking of our missionary task, and especially the ministry aspect of our mission, has brought about several brave attempts in recent years to remobilize the mission of the Church. These attempts have been stimulating, but not always heard or accepted. So often we are fighting the "we have always done it this way" syndrome.

Much of the rethinking for the mission of the Church in small communities has been pursued along the line of new forms of ministries. We have found such rethinking in the nonstipendiary clergy groups: the Michigan Deacons, the Southern Virginia and Saskatchewan "Greater Parish concept," various types of team ministries, many attempts to make available new forms of ministry, and education for that ministry for the laity of the Church. The most thoroughly thought-out course for lay ministry and locally trained clergy has recently come out of the University of the South under the direction of Dr. Charles Winters. This is the method of "theological education by extension," which has been most fruitful in Latin America and, with the adaptations made by Dr. Winters, points to being one of the most beneficial tools to train and inspire the laity of the Church in the mission in which we are all called to partake.

The Commission on the Church in Small Communities, and its whole "New Directions" program under the directorship of the Rev. Dr. Boone Porter, shows much vision and has great potential for mission in the small community. Other movements which have faced reality and looked ahead with vision are those dioceses which have formed coalitions of support and those dioceses which have renewed their deanery structure to better serve the mission and ministry of the Church. However, the temptation is often just to reorganize and to forget the reason for our existence as the people of God. There is a thirst by many of our laity to find an outlet for ministry; they ask for training, but above all for opportunity and direction. The Church must prepare itself to meet this need and allow the whole people of God to be about the work of the Kingdom.

These citings mention only some of the present thinkings and workings, but all have made a contribution to the new direction in which the Church can turn in its mission in the small community. We tend to try to want to organize such thinking so that we can control it; it then loses its "life spark," becomes shackled by the organization, and dies. We give the organizational aspect priority rather than its object, and we lose our impetus and spontaneity.

The untapped evangelistic potential of the people of the Church, for the most part, lies dormant. It is here, in the individual Christian, supported and encouraged by the whole body, that the spearhead of the Church's mission is to be found.

The spontaneous expansion of the Church is impossible or at any rate is severely checked by our refusal to recognize that the apostles knew how to organize the

Church so that it could expand spontaneously and rapidly, and we are simply defeating our own ends by refusing to recognize it.

—Roland Allen

How then is the Church to move this mighty army in the mission of the Church? How do we encourage the laity to be a part of the whole ministry? We must first look to the areas of providing opportunity, encouraging involvement, and deploying the many talents of our people. Given this kind of opportunity and openness, we will then be faced with a need for training and direction. Our somewhat comfortable Episcopalian malaise, clergy dependence, and the pursuit of secondary priorities discourage missionary endeavor. The laity will need time to adjust to their role as part of the mission of the Church, and the clergy will need time to adjust to their role and become enablers rather than doers of all things.

An age of movement of the Spirit is upon us and many of the fruits of this movement are new commitments to our Lord and to mission in the Church. Whether that movement is charismatic, Faith Alive, or Cursillo—to take but a few—a newness of Spirit is emerging which is saying, in essence, that it is not enough to know about Christ, we must know him. And in knowing Christ, spontaneous expansion of the Church should be an obvious fruit, and perhaps will continue to be so in a much fuller way.

The reality of our present situation is such that we have some tools to work with and, if the trap of giving the organization priority can be overcome, these tools can produce great results. To elaborate on this point, let us look at the potential of theological education by extension as it applies to the Church in the small community. We now have at our disposal the means to train our laity for mission and ministry. They can be given the means to teach, preach, and visit sick and potential members. Lay people can also be trained for ordination to celebrate the sacraments in their community and be enabled by seminary trained clergy. The Sewanee course gives opportunity to members of the Church in small communities to minister and to be about our Lord's business. As Ted Ward and Samuel F. Rowen state in their publication "the Significances of the Extension Seminary":

Theological education by extension is not an attempt to make the best of a bad situation. It is part of a worldwide trend based upon substantial research on how people learn. Just why leaders of the Church over the centuries have made so little attempt to understand and appreciate the teaching techniques and environments used by Jesus will likely remain one of the great mysteries. Wesley caught a glimpse of the essence; the Presbyterians in Guatemala in the mid-1960s caught another. Where this 'movement' of theological education by extension (if an educational development can be called a 'movement') has touched, enrollments in

The Church is Small Communities

theological education have multiplied and the educational experiences have taken on a fresh relevancy to the needs of the Church of Jesus Christ.

This approach to mission with the independence it offers churches in small communities has great potential.

Another example which offers much vision and hope is that of "New Directions" which has been briefly touched upon. Here are guidelines which, if implemented, provide aid to the people of God in order to fulfill their mission in the world. The first aspect of New Directions is the recognition of the capacity of lay people to carry out ministry at the local level, and the need to strengthen this capacity with lay theological education. New Directions then points to the potential and recognition of nonstipendiary clergy; regional structures for mutual support of both small and large churches; and the providing of mature, experienced, and well-informed supervisory persons to direct and coordinate regional activities. All aspects of this approach are animated by the conviction that Jesus Christ, the living Lord, can and does work in and through his Church. A theology of the Church as the body of Christ is basic to such renewal and such renewal must involve the whole body. New Directions holds great hope for the future of the Church in the small community; its ideas and the application of those ideas need to be pursued in the future.

An excellent application of this new thinking can be seen in the Church in Alaska, and before it, the Church of South India. Here we see locally chosen and trained clergy who can minister in their own community and bring about stability and expansion of the faith. The early Church certainly used such ministers, who in turn used all the people of God in the mission and ministry of the Church. Allen points to this historical situation and compares it to the Church in this century.

In the early Church we find local men ordained for the local church. They were ordained for that church and they did not seek for some congenial sphere wherever they might see an opening or could obtain preferment. Thus the link between the church and the ministry was maintained. But in our system when the ministry is considered a personal gift, men seek for themselves, or are sent by authority, to occupy this post or that, without regard to the link which is then snapped, and the consequence is that they often look upon "churches" simply as places which offer them opportunities for the exercise of their gifts, or as steps in a ladder of preferment.

In this same context we see bishops who were pastors to their clergy and people, because they knew their people and only had a reasonable number to minister to. Perhaps the day is coming when we should renew the episcopate and expand its pastoral usage by multiplying our shepherds, so that they can indeed be shepherds tending and personally encouraging their flock, instead of being bound down with the administration of a diocese. In the early Church, metropolitans were the administrators of larger geographical areas, while bishops went about their pastoral duties; and the Church prospered and grew on such love and care.

Much could be said about seminarians working for a time in the field, of worker priests, of clergy as enablers, and of the work of nonstipendiary clergy as opposed to those who have "opted out." We are faced with an incredible situation in our Church today, an inability to deploy all our clergy; we call this a clergy surplus. Perhaps our more serious problem is not a surplus of clergy, but a scarcity of laity in ministry. This is particularly true of the Church in small communities, where we have seen that finances, instability, and a lack of job satisfaction have not resulted in fruitful ministry or the expansion of the Church.

Spontaneous expansion as explained by Roland Allen has much to say to us today and his works are worth reading and digesting. The mission of God's people is to bring the good news to all men. We tend to lament our rather staid and stagnant missionary attempt. We need to preach and teach that all God's people are called to be the body of Christ in the world and to act upon our words. The faith we have in Christ brings great joy, a joy to be shared with all men. It is life; and we too often convey by our mission in small communities that it has no life and that we are preservers of a dead faith. The visions given to us today can be realized when we look at the great potential, yet untapped, in the ministry and mission of the whole people of God. Our future task is to awaken this messenger and send it about its work equipped to be the preachers and teachers of Christ in a world ripe for this message of love and hope.

The one thing to be learned is how to live the Christian life in that state and social order in which the Christian finds themselves.

What is needed is the kind of faith which, uniting a man to Christ, sets him on fire.

NOTES

1. Books by Roland Allen: *The Spontaneous Expansion of the Church* (Grand Rapids, Mich.: Wm. B. Eerdmans Co., 1962); *Missionary Methods: St. Paul's or Ours* (Grand Rapids, Mich.: Wm. B. Eerdmans Co., 1962); *The Ministry of the Spirit* (Grand Rapids, Mich.: Wm. B. Eerdmans Co., 1962).

chapter 4

ECUMENISM AND THE CONSULTATION ON CHURCH UNION

John M. Krumm

If you were asked what Church you belonged to, my guess is that you would reply, "I belong to St. Paul's Church, Middletown," naming the congregation where your name is recorded on the rolls. That would be, of course, a correct answer; but if you think about it, you will realize that it is not really a full and complete answer. Perhaps you would answer, "I belong to the Episcopal Church—or the Anglican Communion—and my congregational affiliation is St. Paul's Church, Middletown." That would be more complete as an answer, and yet it is still not an altogether full and adequate answer. I wonder how many of us would think to answer something like this: "I belong to the Holy Catholic Church of Jesus Christ, to that branch of it known as the Anglican Communion or the Episcopal Church in the United States, and my congregational affiliation is with St. Paul's Church in Middletown." I confess that if a casual questioner received that kind of answer, he might regret ever having brought the subject up in the first place, but that would be the only fully satisfactory answer to the question "What Church do you belong to?" One way to describe the so-called ecumenical movement is that it is promoting that kind of answer to that particular question.

My guess is that it is precisely because so few Christian people think to answer that way that so much of the Church's life is marked by apathy and lack of enthusiasm, and that the commitment of so many Church people is only a token sort. If our perspective is narrowed down to the limits of our present congregation, we miss much of the excitement of God's great purpose in bringing the Church into being. If all we think of when we hear the word "church" is our own immediate congregation—important, essential, and precious as that relationship is—then we miss the dramatic concept of the Church in the creeds as an ages-old and worldwide fellowship, a multitude which no one can number, out of every race and nation and language, drawn more closely together than any other fellowship on earth. That sets our own individual congregation in a wonderful perspective, and we need that perspective no matter what the state of the local congregation may be.

If we are in a large and bustling parish, well-financed, well-organized, possessed of many members, and growing week by week (are there such congregations anymore?), the danger is that we shall become complacent and self-congratulatory. If, on the other hand, our local congregation is hard-pressed, small, poor, struggling, losing more members every time a new controversy sweeps through our thinning ranks, then the obvious danger is that we shall lose heart and perhaps desert the seemingly sinking ship.

In either case, what a stimulus it would be if we could see the life of our own congregation in the setting of the Holy Catholic Church throughout all the world, realizing that we worship and pray and act out our discipleship to Christ in company with an unseen but exciting host of men and women from every generation: heroes and heroines of the faith; pioneers of Christ's Spirit in unpromising places and times; martyrs, missionaries, clergy, laity, monks, scholars; and all the rest who have been drawn to Christ in love and trust and who seek to serve and bear witness to him. To see in our imagination this great experiment in human community which God has launched and which he has called us to share as the background and context for the life of an individual congregation—this, I believe, would do much to revive and renew the Church.

I confess this vision takes faith and hope. So much of our Church life seems to make a mockery of the great adjectives which the creeds use to describe the Church—"One, Holy, Catholic, and Apostolic." The religion sections of the Saturday newspapers, with the announcements and advertisements of Sunday worship services, loudly proclaim this lack of oneness. Here are scores of Christian bodies living more or less in isolation from one another, in some cases anathematizing and excommunicating one another. Nor are they conspicuously holy, aflame with the passion of God for righteousness, for the fulfillment of each man and woman in their dignity as children of God. How can we describe the Church as Catholic when so often the limit of its concerns is the boundaries of a single congregation, its buildings, and its ministry to its own members and no one else? How "Catholic" is a budget that allocates only a fraction of its income for the mission of the Church in a diocese, nation, and world?

How can we claim the word "Apostolic" for a Church that lacks the zeal and the self-sacrifice and the boldness which marked so dramatically the first days of the Church's life? No, this is why the Church is mentioned in the creed. We must *believe* in it as well as belong to it. We must see it whole in the parish we live in, with the great experiment of God in drawing people together across all the barriers that separate them. That takes faith and hope in large measure. To help us judge and measure the Church as it is in our congregations and dioceses, we keep rehearsing, in the creeds, what we believe about the Church.

Even in the Church as it is, however, we catch glimpses of the possibility that this vision of hope and faith is not illusory but has some ground and basis. I see one such glimpse in the continuation in the Church of the apostolic role of the bishop. I am struck, in reading the epistles of St. Paul, by the way he drew the tiny congregations scattered all over the Roman Empire into a single communion and fellowship. He traveled over the Mediterranean world to visit all the little house churches which he had created by his preaching and teaching, and it was he who kept them close to one another, contributing to the relief of one another's necessities. His letters reflect this: "Greetings from the congregations in Asia." "All the brethren here greet you." "All Christ's congregations send you their greetings." He alone could speak for "all Christ's congregations," for he alone knew them all, prayed for them all, counseled and advised them all. So he was a sign and a mark of their catholicity.

The role of the bishop is one of the difficult questions facing any discussion of Church union, and the Consultation on Church Union (COCU) is no exception. As this essay is being written, a "Commission on the Revision of the Theological Basis for the Church" of COCU is at work on a document which will include a chapter on ministry in which the question of the role of the episcopacy in a projected "Church of Christ Uniting" will be dealt with. How satisfactory this forthcoming statement will be remains to be seen, but the Episcopalians in COCU are committed, in loyalty to the Lambeth Quadrilateral, to the maintenance of the episcopacy as an essential token and effectual sign of the catholicity and apostolicity of the Church.

The details of the bishop's power and responsibility are not, of course, at issue. Those details have changed throughout the long history of the Church and no doubt can undergo further change without destroying the pastoral and unifying role that Episcopalians hold to be crucial in the bishop's commission and task. Other Christian bodies in the Consultation are open, I am convinced, to an acceptance of this kind of an episcopate in a united Church.

Another glimpse can be discerned within the present structure and life of the Church—even in its divided state—in a common deposit of faith and practice. The Holy Scriptures, the traditional creeds as expressing the major teaching of the Scriptures, the two dominical sacraments—on these crucial matters there is general agreement revealed in the COCU discussions. This fact makes the present ecumenical situation different from that of previous times, when the divisions within Christendom marked substantial doctrinal differences on major features of Christian faith. There will no doubt always be shades of difference in theological teaching and understanding in the Christian Church, but unless these differences touch essential doctrines they need not be barriers to a genuinely unified Church.

On any given Sunday one can imagine the kind of diversity of settings and situations in which the same Scriptures are being read, the same sacraments of baptisms and holy communion are being administered, and the same essential faith is being taught in preaching and expressed in prayer and worship. In a grass hut on a Pacific island, in a crowded refugee center in Hong Kong, behind closed doors under threat of totalitarian persecution, in magnificent ceremonial and architectural splendor in St. Peter's Basilica in Rome, in a simple colonial style church in a New England village—all sorts and conditions of people are already expressing the same faith in Christ and receiving the promise and power of his love and presence. The ecumenical movement, including the Consultation on Church Union, does not seek to impose some novelty on the Christian Churches. It seeks only to make more visible a reality already discernible for those who have eyes to see—that there is one Holy, Catholic, and Apostolic Church "throughout all the world."

The Consultation on Church Union has not yet produced a satisfactory blueprint of the organizational structure by which a united Church could live and function, and there are signs that this may require a major effort of imagination and an almost miraculous inspiration of divine wisdom. There are some who question the importance of this part of the ecumenical movement, wondering whether a mutual recognition of ordained ministries in the separated Churches and a consequent intercommunion among them might not be sufficient. One way to evaluate this more modest ecumenical proposal in the Episcopal Church situation is to ask what our own Church would be like if, in a given geographical area, there were no structure by which we carried on mission and witness but were content simply to share a bishop in common. We would have intercommunion and a mutual recognition of ministry but no coming together, no sharing of insights or understandings of the meaning and significance of the Gospel. This does not fulfill the picture our Lord drew of the unity of the Church in the high priestly prayer in John 17:21: "That they all may be one; as thou, Father, art in me, and I in thee, that they may also be one in us."

Bishop Leslie Newbigin once described the pastoral situation in the congregations of the newly united Church of South India. Formerly, when there were several competing congregations of different denominational traditions in a single village or town, a disgruntled or disaffected Church member could simply take leave of one congregation and move to another. However, when these several congregations drew together in a closely shared life of worship, work, and witness, that luxury of seeking out a more comfortable or congenial congregation was eliminated. In the newly unified congregations of the Church of South India the full meaning of Christian unity had to be worked out in some resolution of differences and some reconciliation of styles of Christian life. That task of reconciliation in the several congregations of the Church of South India became one of the bishop's more demanding responsibilities. Mere mutual recognition of ministries and intercommunion between otherwise separated Church bodies, while it would mark significant ecumenical advance, would appear to fall short of the close sharing and intimate fellowship implied in the Lord's high priestly prayer.

Ever since the Memphis Plenary of 1973, the Consultation on Church Union has sought to launch local experiments in shared mission and eucharistic worship among the nine COCU Churches—and others willing to join them. The purpose is not to achieve a kind of end-run around stubborn differences of conviction, especially about the forms of ministry. It is rather to uncover areas of agreement and consensus on matters of theology and practice which can guide the leadership of COCU, and to provide experiences of Christian community across the traditional divisions of the Christian Church which have proved so formidable in the past. It must be confessed that these local experiments have not been altogether successful. The number of places where a real coming together has been possible have been few. Most frequently it is not deep theological differences that have kept the separated Churches apart but something far less respectable—narrow denominational pride and jealous autonomy.

An advertisement on the church page of a Miami newspaper a few months ago carried an announcement of services at a local church identifiable as a dissenting congregation formerly part of the local diocese of the Episcopal Church. At the bottom of the advertisement were these words: "This church belongs to no Council of Churches." What a tragic display of fear and anxiety and clannishness! What a sad failure to make any effort to fulfill the Lord's purpose for a Catholic, worldwide fellowship! Here is a congregation either too insecure or too complacent to share in any way in mission and witness with other Christian bodies with different styles in worship, different perceptions of the Church's role in the world, different ways of expressing the faith of the Scriptures and of Christian tradition. This timidity and narrow self-satisfaction is the enemy of ecumenism, more powerful than any deeply theological issues. This is the kind of sin for which the Churches are called to repentance and renewal.

The Episcopal Church's General Convention in September of 1976 will be asked to accept as a basis for ecumenical concern and activity a statement of the Consultation on Church Union on "Mutual Recognition of Membership." This statement plainly repeats what the Episcopal Church has said in its catechism—that all persons baptized with water in the name of the Trinity share in a common membership in the Church of Jesus Christ. "What is the Church?" asks the Office of Instruction in the 1928 Book of Common Prayer, and the answer is absolutely clear: "The Church is the Body of which Jesus Christ is the Head and *all baptized persons are the members.*" (Emphasis mine.)

As the statement goes on to make clear, this is the platform for all ecumenical activity. It does not ignore the fact that at this moment our membership in Christ's Holy Catholic Church is nurtured and lived out in a special ecclesial body called the Episcopal Church, but it recognizes that this participation in the life of the Episcopal Church ought never to obscure the more fundamental truth—that we share in the larger life of that blessed company of all faithful people who by baptism have been incorporated into Christ. What can we do to manifest more openly and visibly this larger association and identification? The ecumenical movement seeks to provide suggested answers to that question.

At the present time, from all the evidence, the Episcopal Church is more intrigued with the new openness and receptivity to ecumenical gestures and advances with the Roman Catholic Church. This is obviously exciting, and a development for which we should all be overwhelmingly grateful to God. But Anglicanism has always maintained a sense of close association with the Churches of the Reformation of the sixteenth century. The Consultation on Church Union represents nine such bodies. All evidence points to the fact that these bodies are ready and willing to discuss in great sympathy and seriousness the marks of apostolicity and catholicity identified in the Lambeth Quadrilateral, including the office of the bishop as continuing to fulfill the role of the apostles in the Church of the New Testament. Efforts to withdraw the Episcopal Church from such discussions reflect the kind of isolationism which, as we have seen above, is the enemy of all genuine ecumenism. No serious theological issue is involved in the acceptance of the statement on "Mutual Recognition of Membership." If other statements are proposed in COCU negotiations, they will be carefully scrutinized by the Episcopal Church's representatives to the negotiations, as well as by the whole Joint Commission on Ecumenical Relations. There is every reason for confidence that nothing will be done hastily or in a way that repudiates the Lambeth Quadrilateral. Fears of what may result from participation in the COCU discussions are quite baseless.

The whole ecumenical outreach of the Church in these days must be viewed against the background of the search of our contemporary world for some hope that there is a way around the hostilities and antagonisms and barriers which today, in so many parts of the world, are causing acute suffering and death. Are we in the Churches able to overcome our excessive fears and timidity, and to reach out in dramatic and convincing ways to show the world more clearly that the true basis of human solidarity is our common dependence on God's mercy, God's love, God's grace? That we all need his forgiveness, his vision, his power is the assumption which underlies all Christian worship, the sacraments, prayer, the Christian life. Nothing less than the great Church of the creeds—One, Holy, Catholic, and Apostolic—can give an adequate witness to the world of the reality of that assumption and its reconciling power. In this perspective, ecumenism is one of the Church's central, crucial, and urgent priorities.

chapter 5

ANGLICAN AND ROMAN CATHOLIC

Jean Henkel Johnson

    Force us to let ourselves say something that helps and heals, that sets right and builds up.
    —Hugo Sonderegger[1]

The present is a fulcrum. Can the realities of the future be lifted up to the visions of the past? What of Anglican-Roman Catholic relations? More immediately and particularly: What kinship is there between American Roman Catholicism and the "Protestant Episcopal Church in the United States of America, otherwise known as the Episcopal Church"?[2] What can be predicted? What can be looked forward to? The prophetic word is always disconcerting—to the prophet, disturbing, since projection often sounds an unfamiliar scale of tones; to the hearer, confusing his comfort or diminishing to *stentando* his listening for *staccato*. What can be foreseen? The speculations of any prophet may be only looking in a cloudy glass or with astigmatic vision.

What, then? Insistent challenge. The discipline of decision. The conversion of consultation into active joint ministry to the eager, the indifferent, and the bewildered of God's world. Risk! Or a loss of confidence through fear that tradition, often already unauthentic, and institution, already insecure, are threatened. This decade may reach that point of decision at which the Church will either embark on ecumenical adventure under the command of the Spirit or retire from that enterprise urged by our Lord: "Go into all the world."

On December 11, 1969, the Joint Anglican-Roman Catholic Commission, U.S.A. (ARC), sent greetings to the Permanent Commission for Anglican-Roman Catholic International Relations (now known as ARCIC)[3] which was about to hold its initial meeting at Windsor, England. The salutation from the American commission expressed a "sense of the importance and *urgency* of the common task." It continued with the assurance of an *"urgent* will to achieve . . . the reconciliation of Anglicans and Roman Catholics as also to promote the wider unity of all Christians in their common Lord."[4] This note of urgency had also been sounded in the Report of the Joint Preparatory Commission. It had described its meetings as "characterized not only by a spirit of charity and frankness, but also by a growing sense of *urgency* . . . of *urgency* in response to the pressure of God's will, apprehended as well in the processes of history and the aspirations and achievements of men in his world as in the life, worship, witness, and service of his Church."[5]

There was a cheering flash of Pentecost when the aim was stated of "firing" the people of the two Churches to engage in this commitment. This was 1969. Now it is the mid-1970s. Has the fire been banked through the period of theological and ecclesiological study in consultations? There has been a sniff of suspicion that initial enthusiasm is smoldering. Are there any spurts of flame?

Current ecumenical concern expresses itself in "yearning." The word has changed, but desire is implicit whether in "urgency" or "yearning." It is not only talked about in parley, it is being communicated through visible signs.

Reports from the second annual meeting of Episcopal Diocesan Ecumenical Officers (EDEO) in February 1976 are lively and insistent. They celebrate "commitment to local ecumenism." As of that date there were ecumenical officers in ninety-two of the ninety-three domestic dioceses. Replies from sixty-five dioceses to a questionnaire, when tabulated, showed "ARC an overwhelming priority in interest." This interest roused these questions: "What are they doing that is right? What can we learn from ARC?"[6]

The Anglican-Roman Catholic Consultation, U.S.A., emerged from a resolution of General Convention pertaining to ecumenical dialogue. The Episcopalians on the consultation represent the Joint Commission on Ecumenical Relations of the Episcopal Church (JCER). The Roman Catholic members are representatives of the Bishops' Commission for Ecumenical and Interreligious Affairs. ARC is one of the now many bilateral dialogues between Christian denominations. The latest edition of *Confessions in Dialogue*[7] describes nearly fifty such ecumenical consultations and notes their rapid growth during the last decade. Since 1965 the Anglican-Roman Catholic Commission has engaged in theological inquiry resulting in consensus papers on baptism, the Eucharist, and ministry. Its present and future agenda show increasing concern for local ecumenism among the people of God and for the pastoral aspects of full communion.

If a decade of theological dialogue seems to have slowed down the expectation of action roused by the early expressions of urgency, there have, however, been reports of Anglican-Roman Catholic cooperation elsewhere that strides ahead of the present stance of what, in the way of official action, the work of either ARC (U.S.A.) or ARCIC has been able to further.

One of these reports is of the activity of the Masasi section of East African ARC which:

. . . has produced a joint religious education syllabus, translated the Canterbury Statement [on ministry and ordination] into Swahili, and is working on a project for a common Lord's Prayer, Creed and Gloria, a significant step because Swahili is the common language in Tanzania, Kenya, Uganda, Mozambique and Zaire.[8]

Such recognition of joint responsibility in meeting the reality of common need is a worthwhile response to ecumenical vision. It replies to urgency. It indicates directions for future ecumenical development in showing how one kind of model of unity can be constructed out of a desire for shared liturgy and the recognition of sensible procedures for common religious instruction. (Is the joint syllabus a hint of a novel application of "the Teaching Authority of the Church"—simple *Magisterium* at the independent regional level?)

On January 18, 1970, at Great St. Mary's Church in Cambridge, England, Cardinal Jan Willebrands, the wise Roman Catholic ecumenist, described the Christian Church as a *typos* (Greek: a form, figure, image, or impression) and suggested that denominational communities exist as *typoi* within the Christian *typos*. (Christianity itself would be one of the *typoi* within the *typos* of world religion—others being Judaism, Islam, Buddhism, and Hinduism.) Closer kinships exist between certain of the *typoi* constituting the *typos* than among others. This can produce natural combinations.

In consultation, ARC, prompted by Willebrands's suggestion, has tried to use this system of *typoi* within *typos* as a device "for guiding analytical thinking about relationships between the Roman Catholic and Episcopal Churches in the United States." This has been done with the expectation that "it may offer a means for identifying the attributes essential to the mutual recognition of a substantially shared status as components of the organic whole of the general system of the Church Universal."[9] The Masasi ARC model of recognized practical need and shared elements of liturgy illustrates the effectiveness of like attributes in combining *typoi* to form a new unit. Note also the factor of common language.

An example of another model of subsystem unity is to be found in the Declaration of the Church of South India, the Church of North India, and the Mar Thoma Syrian Church of Malabar. These Churches are members of the Wider Episcopal Fellowship. The recommendations of the declaration look toward embodying within structure—that is, in unification—their already existing unity in theological agreement and eucharistic fellowship. Institutional unification is expected to further practical projects of service. Note here the factor of geographical situation.

In what viable model of unity is the Episcopal Church likely to feel the most congeniality? In what will it provide unique attributes essential for promoting wider unity? Will the relations of Churches in the Wider Episcopal Fellowship with other Christian denominations affect Episcopal-Roman Catholic positions on full communion and validity of orders? Bilateral conversations suggest clues to affinities, diversities, and genuine differences.

Advances in theological agreement deriving from dialogue, incidents of cooperation in ministry, and continuing expressions of desire for shared worship encourage ecumenical expectation. But there must be no blindness to failures of plans and retreats into moratoria. What has conditioned defeat and delay?

In the experience of dialogue there is the immediate factor of language. Before discussion can have authentic meaning, the connotations that words carry must be questioned and agreement reached. Even among persons speaking the same language, words become "loaded" with prejudice. Across geographical, ethnic, and denominational lines misunderstanding is magnified. Special interest groups develop an argot of their own. In response to complaints of "ecumenical jargon," a brief lexicon was included in the World Council of Churches publication, *Uppsala to Nairobi*, in preparation for the 1975 Assembly.[10]

Beyond this basic level of ecumenical communication there exists the problem of theological implication and interpretation. In admitting this as applying directly to Anglican-Roman Catholic Consultation, Cardinal Willebrands said, "A common declaration of faith on points which have been controversial during four centuries supposes a creative work concerning language and expression."[11] He further quoted the declaration of the Second Vatican Council:

The manner and order in which Catholic belief is expressed should in no way become an obstacle to dialogue. . . . At the same time, Catholic belief needs to be explained more profoundly and precisely, in ways which our separated brethren too can really understand. *(Unitatis Redintegratio* 11.)[12]

As dialogue moves into the difficult areas ot papacy, primacy, Petrine doctrine, and Marian dogma, theological vocabulary must be explicit and its interpretation in common speech meticulous. As for Episcopalians, do they know what they are hearing and what they themselves are saying? Can we understand our own theologians? Can we translate into basic American? The use of words demands art and skill. (It is exciting, too; otherwise there would be no crossword puzzles.) Why not some semantic team play? The Episcopal Church could gather in colloquia its theologians, church historians, linguistic analysts, liturgiologists, authors, actors, preachers, media experts, common readers, and laity of plain speech. Consultation consensus papers could spark definition, argument, and interpretation.

Who do men say that we are? Who do we say that we are? Our tradition merits accurate description. It can be neither defended nor amended if not truly understood. In writing of tradition, Philip Sherrard has said:

One's primary loyalty and faith must be directed towards one's own tradition, and to deepening one's experience of that. If one is concerned with other traditions, one must seek to understand them as fully as one can from within, being careful not to pre-judge or to interpret them in the light of principles derived from some exterior point of view.[13]

No one can comprehend in dialogue another's tradition without being conversant with one's own. Tradition is not a legacy of legend. It speaks to today's questions out of the wisdom of experience. It should rouse convictions. These deserve sharp and precise declaration, for ecumenism rightly prizes independence as well as agreement.

Shared tradition has often been accredited as a primary factor toward organic unity in Anglican-Roman Catholic relations. Common liturgy is held to be an essential attribute in the forming of any viable religious subsystem. Massey H. Shepherd, Jr., reporting as an observer at Vatican II, said in 1967:

We [Anglicans and Roman Catholics] have both affirmed and experienced through the liturgy that unity of faith in the bond of peace which is the peculiar treasure of the Missal and Breviary on the one hand, and of the Book of Common Prayer on the other. Now it seems possible to envisage a reconciliation in worship, which derives not only from a common origin, but from agreement in basic principles.[14]

He also points out, however:

There are, to be sure, obstacles other than liturgical worship which have separated us: theological and institutional differences, not to speak of psychological and cultural variances of temper and behavior.[15]

On October 4, 1972, Cardinal Willebrands, lecturing in the Great Hall of Lambeth Palace, emphasized the spiritual nature of ecumenical relationships but observed also matters of practical difficulty. He is too aware

Anglican and Roman Catholic

and too honest not to admit these as serious realities even as he has rejoiced in fraternal response and has envisioned true unity. In conclusion he said:

Organic unity is based upon faith. . . . The root of our division lies there. . . . We are still divided in matters of faith, there is our greatest difficulty. . . . Since it is a task of theology to explain to us the content of our faith . . . we are grateful for every effort made by theologians for the cause of unity.[16]

ARC had come into being as just such a theological task force. This commission has been diligent in the study of pertinent documents, open in discussion, and devoted to the desire for unity. Very early in the course of consultation there was agreement on baptism. At the first meeting of the commission, June 1965, there was agreement "that the instances of conditional baptism of Episcopalians for admission to the Roman Catholic Church . . . were abuses."[17] In 1964 the House of Bishops of the Episcopal Church had proposed to General Convention a resolution for the admission of all baptized communicant members of other Churches to communion in the Episcopal Church. The House of Deputies did not then convene. Study by a theological committee was asked. As a result of this study it was announced in March 1967 that the Joint Commission on Ecumenical Relations would report to the House of Bishops that such admission to communion would require no canonical or rubrical change. In May 1967 ARC stated: "Baptism is the entrance into Eucharistic community."[18] There is no obstacle to full communion because of initiatory impediment.

ARC, therefore, then proceeded to careful study of the theology of the Eucharist. It issued its first statement in May 1967, the opening paragraph of which reads:

Since the time of the Reformation the doctrine of Eucharistic sacrifice has been considered a major obstacle to the reconciliation of the Anglican Communion and the Roman Catholic Church. It is the conviction of our Commission that this is no longer true.[19]

In 1971, ARCIC concluded its Agreed Statement on Eucharistic Doctrine thus:

We believe that we have reached substantial agreement on the doctrine of the Eucharist . . . we are convinced that if there are any remaining points of disagreement they can be resolved on the principles here established.[20]

Both the international commission and the American commission, after long and thorough study, were able to make consensus statements. The theological consultants had agreed both on baptism and on eucharistic sacrifice and fellowship. The agreed statements were forwarded to the appropriate offices. They were "received with appreciation." Doctrinal obstacles had been removed. The Episcopal Church had opened its Holy Communion to Christians in good standing. There has been no change in the Roman Catholic officially discriminate celebration of the Eucharist. The goal of full communion, long anticipated, remains a vision. A decade is done; another decade is beginning.

A great company were gathered. They had come from many places. They were hungry but they trusted the companionship of One in whom they believed. He stood among them and, looking toward that place where traditionally the glory of the Lord shone, He said: "Blessed is the Lord our God, Ruler of the Universe, Who causes bread to come forth from the earth. Blessed is the Lord our God, Ruler of the Universe, Creator of the fruit of the vine."

And He took bread and broke it, and He poured out wine. Then He called to the company to count off from one through twelve. There was some confusion. Turning to one named Simon whom He called Peter, He said, "Take those numbered one down by the sea and give them to eat." Turning to one named Andrew, He said, "You were first, but you have always loved and preferred your brother. Take those numbered two and climb the hill northward." To James and John He said with a smile, "Take your four hundreds and go off to my right or my left hand. If you cannot decide which, ask your mother, for she knows where you should be." To Thomas He said, "You and your handful can inquire and search out a place." Turning to Judas He said, "Yonder is a tree and beyond it a field. Take there with you your company. Yours are the bewildered who yet give their lives in penitence. Rest there forgiven. Hear the comfortable words."

So they separated and went their divided ways.

The children too young to count, what of them? There came along a Greek named Nicholas. The children being too young for bread and wine, bless them, and this being a land of milk and honey, perhaps with Nicholas and the lamb and the bees they could find sweet sustenance. And Jesus said, "Don't send them away." He liked them around him.

A fable. It does not have the authority of Scripture.

What future, then, can be expected to eventuate from consensus statements such as those on baptism and eucharistic doctrine? In 1968, ARC defined its bounds:

The Joint Anglican-Roman Catholic Consultation recognizes that it can make only recommendations, not decisions. . . . Such decisions must be arrived at by the appropriate authorities of each Church after consideration and recommendation by our parent bodies.[21]

The Faith and Order Commission of the World Council of Churches spoke to the use of agreed statements as a vital part of a process:

It is from the life and thought of the People of God that the consensus emerges and it is into that life that it must be fed back. . . . The consensus is addressed to at least three groups—theologians, church leaders, and the faithful in general. . . . Theologians are stimulated to new encounters, church leaders given a basis for decision-making and the faithful in general encouraged to deepen their Christian living together.[22]

The faithful are frequently to be seen practicing their Christian living together, often without sanction, sometimes with a nonchalance to censure. The people of God are questioning together, studying together, singing together. A fire is edging through the grass roots. One form of this conflagration is the covenant relationship into which a growing number of Episcopal and Roman Catholic parishes have entered "in order to promote fraternal relations and to signify willingness to move toward organic union."[23] The flame is readying the field for new planting. It has reached the attention of Church leaders.

To what new doctrinal encounter were the theologians next stimulated? Ministry was now on the agenda of both Anglican-Roman Catholic consultations. Again consensus statements have resulted. In making public the ARCIC Canterbury Statement in 1973, it was stated:

The Commission is reporting to the authorities who appointed it on one of the items on its program of work. These authorities have allowed the Statement to be published so that it may be discussed by other theologians. It is not a declaration by the Roman Catholic Church or by the Anglican Communion. It does not authorize any change in existing ecclesiastical discipline.[24]

The conclusion of the statement records an awareness "of the issues raised by the judgment of the Roman Catholic Church on Anglican Orders" and admits that "the wide-ranging problems of authority [and] the question of primacy" have not yet been broached.[25] Both commissions are working on these issues. The use of language again arises to cause confusion. Much of the discussion must be intramural in order to determine the contemporary Roman Catholic position. Anglicans must wait and trust the Roman Catholic theologians to agree on basic definitions and value judgments so that true translation of these can be made and right interpretation given. This is of special importance in the Episcopal Church because of the authority of lay delegates in the General Convention.

What of the troubling question of the validity of Anglican Orders? The Canterbury Statement summarizes: "Agreement on the nature of Ministry is prior to the consideration of the mutual recognition of ministries."[26]

What, on best authority, is "the nature of Ministry"? Let us remind ourselves of our living Lord, God incarnate, at the initiation of his ministry in time and place. He went into the congregation and took the scroll of Scripture and read:

> The spirit of the Lord God is upon me,
> For the Lord has anointed me;
> He has sent me to bring good news . . .
> To mend the broken,
> To proclaim liberty to captives
> And release to the bound,
> To announce the year of God's good will
> And the day of God's judgment.[27]

He went out to give glory to a ministry of doing justice, of loving mercy, and of walking rightly with God.[28] This is the nature of Christian ministry. Has the Anglican Communion subscribed to any other? What is validity as witnessed to in the living ministry of our Lord? What does the Lord require? Ecclesiastical discipline and structure are not for the sake of sacerdotal security. Structure of whatever model is to facilitate the life-giving work of the Holy Spirit. In the house of reconciliation, where structure obstructs the Spirit, walls must go down.

The present may be a pause in official Anglican-Roman Catholic relations. But waiting can be expectancy and growth. Long gestation follows the excitement of conception, for new life is developing. There follows the pain of giving up what has been protected. Then the exploration of free relationship begins. While waiting for decisions to be made that fall outside its jurisdiction and for authority to be exerted to end discriminate practice, the Episcopal Church has opportunity for authentic rediscovery of self. Among "the gifts and graces of each segment of the Christian community," what uniqueness does it offer? The Churches of the Anglican Communion have been recognized for "their reverent worship, their Catholic heritage and Protestant conscience, their ecumenical zeal and desire to be used as a house of reconciliation."[29] Do we so see ourselves?

In the gracious house of reconciliation, Father God and Mother Church surely embrace many children. Along with that "warmth of feeling" as "beloved sister" with the older brothers, what do Episcopalians share with the several younger siblings? Even while carrying on the look of the Anglican genes, the Episcopal Church is young, being first generation in a new land. There is the grace of independence as well as the gift of tradition.

Our tradition is to be prized, but our heritage of experience in liturgy we have been counseled to invest and add interest and share, not to wrap up in a fair linen cloth and hold in reserve: "The ritual of the Christian Church, and its founder, Jesus, are powers ready to hand for the seizing again of not only our own authenticity, but simplicity and wholeness in a supermarket world."[30]

Said to be "worldly," why should the Episcopal Church not reach out to the secular? "It is no longer possible for Christians simply to deplore the process of secularization; they have to understand it."[31] Pray God we are not so conformed as to fear the provisional character of life. "Free play in the secular requires the deepening of roots in the revealed. . . . Both the freedom and the discipline are rooted in a religious relation to the living Christ."[32] From this relationship we can bring to ecumenism "a sense of confidence and creativity as well as a sense of playfulness and a willingness to try the impossible."[33] We are told that God played with Wisdom in designing the world.[34]

Risk is a certainty in the future of ecumenism, for it is only so that faith declares itself and the relationship of God and the people of God is confirmed.

Let there be no faulting of realities or visions; the realities are dynamic, the visions glorious.

Deliver us from our narrowmindedness, from our bitterness, from our prejudices. Teach us to recognize the gifts of thy grace amongst all those who call upon thee. Deepen our faithfulness to thy Word, and keep us clear-sighted and open-minded by thy guiding hand. Do not allow us to be led astray by visions which we have conjured up ourselves, nor wander rashly into ways that are not thine. By thy power, O Lord, gather up thy scattered flock under the sole guidance of thy Son, that thy bountiful purpose may be fulfilled and the world may know thee, the one true God, and him whom thou has sent, Jesus Christ.[35]

NOTES

1. In *Sammle dein Volk zur Einheit:* Ökumenische Gebete der Christenheit. Hrsg. von der Gemeinsamen Arbeitsgruppe der Romisch-katholischen Kirche und des Ökumenischen Rats der Kirchen. Freiburg, usw.: Herder, 1971, Nr. 13, S. 16. (German version of an ecumenical collection of prayers assembled at the request of the Joint Working Group of the World Council of Churches and the Roman Catholic Church.) Translation by David E. Johnson.

2. *Constitution and Canons for . . . the Episcopal Church.* (n.p.) Printed for the Convention, 1970, p. 1.

3. This international commission came into being through proposals of the Malta Report produced by the Anglican-Roman Catholic Joint Preparatory Commission in 1967, following upon its meetings at Gazzada, Huntercombe, and Malta. The report is published among *Documents on Anglican-Roman Catholic Relations,* assembled for the Lambeth Conference of 1968 (hereafter cited as "Lambeth 1968"), (n.p., n.d.), pp. 5–11.

4. Letter of ARC VII, December 9, 1969. Circulated in photocopy by the Bish-

ops' Committee for Ecumenical and Interreligious Affairs, January 1970. Emphasis added.

5. Lambeth 1968, p. 5.

6. *Ecumenical Bulletin,* issued by the Ecumenical Office of the Episcopal Church, No. 16, March–April 1976, p. 2.

7. *Confessions in Dialogue,* a Survey of Bilateral Conversations among World Confessional Families 1959–1974, edited by Nils Ehrenström and Günther Gassmann. Geneva: World Council of Churches, 1975.

8. *Ecumenical Bulletin,* No. 15, January-February 1976, p. 22.

9. From an unpublished paper by George A. Shipman, "Notes on the Ideas of *Typos* and *Typoi* as Applied to the Christian Church," prepared for ARC XII and based on general systems theory.

10. *Uppsala to Nairobi,* edited by David Enderton Johnson. (New York: Friendship Press, 1975), pp. 243–250.

11. Cardinal Jan Willebrands: "Prospects for Anglican-Roman Catholic Relations" in *Documents on Anglican Roman Catholic Relations II* (hereafter cited as ARC/DOC II). Washington: United States Catholic Conference Publications Office, 1973, p. 64.

12. Willebrands, *op. cit.*

13. Philip Sherrard: "The Tradition and the Traditions: The Confrontation of Religious Doctrines," *Religious Studies,* Vol. 10, No. 4, p. 417 (Cambridge University Press).

14. *The Second Vatican Council: Studies by Eight Anglican Observers,* ed. Bernard C. Pawley. (London and New York: Oxford University Press, 1967), p. 159.

15. *Loc. cit.*

16. ARC/DOC II, p. 73.

17. Reported in "ARC VII Statement" in *Documents on Anglican/Roman Catholic Relations* (hereafter cited as ARC/DOC I). Washington: United States Catholic Conference, 1972, p. 9.

18. *Ibid.,* Appendix I, p. 21.

19. *Ibid.,* p. 3.

20. *Ibid.,* p. 50.

21. Minutes of ARC VI, December 2–5, 1968, p. 5. Circulated in photocopy.

22. World Council of Churches, Commission on Faith and Order: Document FO/74:16, January 1974, "The Unity of the Church—Next Steps," prepared for the 1974 meeting of the commission. Reprinted in *Mid-Stream,* Vol. XIV No. 1, January 1975.

23. *Ecumenical Bulletin,* September-October 1973, p. 4.

24. *Ministry and Ordination:* A Statement on the Doctrine of the Ministry Agreed by the Anglican/Roman Catholic International Commission, Canterbury, 1973 (hereafter cited as "Canterbury Statement"). (London: S.P.C.K., 1973), p. 24.

25. Canterbury Statement 17, p. 11. Reprinted in the *Anglican Theological Review,* Vol. LVII No. 1, January 1975, p. 100.

26. *Loc. cit.*

27. Isaiah 61:1f., author's translation; cf. Luke 4:16–19.

28. Cf. Micah 6:8.

29. From a litany prepared for the opening service of the North American preparatory meeting for the Fifth Assembly of the World Council of Churches, East Lansing, Michigan, April 20, 1975. Based upon a litany prepared by the (former) Federal Council of Churches.

30. Robert M. Cooper and W. Taylor Stevenson: Introduction to "Prayer, Ritual, and Spiritual Life: a Consultation," *Anglican Theological Review*, Supplementary Series No. 5, June 1975, p. 8.

31. Leslie Newbigin: *Honest Religion for Secular Man*. (Philadelphia: The Westminster Press, 1966), p. 19.

32. *Ibid.*, p. 145.

33. Frank and Theresa Caplan: *The Power of Play*. (Garden City, N.Y.: Anchor Press/Doubleday, 1974), p. 234.

34. Cf. Proverbs 8:22–31, esp. 22a and 30c-31a.

35. Liturgy of the Reformed Church of France. In *La prière oecuménique*. Recueil composé [par Emmanuel Lanne et Bruno Bürki] à la demande du groupe mixte de travail entre le Conseil oecuménique des Eglises et l'Eglise catholique romaine. Taizé: Les Presses de Taizé, 1970, No. 49, pp. 35–36. (French version of an ecumenical collection of prayers assembled at the request of the Joint Working Group of the World Council of Churches and the Roman Catholic Church.) Translation adapted and augmented by David E. Johnson.

chapter 6

STEWARDSHIP: THE MISSION OF GIVING

Furman C. Stough

This is being written in the belief that it will bring new hope, encouragement, and joy to all of those within our Church who are attempting to deal honestly and openly with the whole question of stewardship; to those who have never considered this dimension of their lives; and to those who have despaired of ever seeing the Church, collectively and individually, come to a point of viable stewardship. What I will share with you comes out of my own experience as a lay person, priest, and bishop in this Church. It is an attempt to bring some good news about the Good News.

The stewardship I am referring to in this paper has to do with the stewardship of money. Like most Episcopalians, the word stewardship inevitably brought to mind the three Ts—time, talent, and treasure, and it seemed to require some kind of mixed response. I was never clear about this, and I do not believe the Church was either. If you sought to measure the response, it became even more difficult—you could be accurate about treasure, less so about time, and almost not at all about talent.

At another level, however, there was even more of a problem. Without ever being confronted with a response in terms of your treasure or money, you could respond in some way in terms of your time and talent, and could rationalize that this was sufficient. Granted, there are some persons within the Church who do not have the financial resources to respond, but this is not true of the vast majority. Because of this, I am convinced that our efforts in stewardship must be directed toward money, and that we need to be clear that this is what we are talking about. My experience has been that until a person deals seriously with this aspect of stewardship, no real growth will occur. Conversely, if this is dealt with first, the whole question of the stewardship of time and talent will fall naturally and easily into place.

And so the Church speaks to us of money, and in doing this it does not have to apologize. Once and for all Jesus established the precedent for us—the one subject in the New Testament to which he most often referred is money. With great feeling and openness he constantly addressed the issue, knowing that it contained the potential for the greatest good and the greatest evil.

In our western culture today money is the prime expression of our value system; so much so for the affluent segment that it has become the modern day "sacrament." By it human relationships, institutions, and associations are judged and categorized. It is *the* dynamic factor that operates in our society.

In the face of this, there are strong signs throughout the Church that constructive and creative efforts are being made to bring the Gospel to bear on this issue and to break open for us the good news that is caught up in the Christian doctrine of stewardship. Representative of these efforts is the work being done on the parish and diocesan levels by such persons as Ebert Hobbs in Ohio, Bill Caradine and Jim Sanders in Alabama, and George Regas in California. Theologians of the Church—in the persons of Michael Allen at Berkeley, Robert Cooper at Nashotah, and Fitz Allison in New York—are giving creature substance to the theological and biblical structures on which our concept of stewardship hangs. At the national Church level, Oscar Carr and his Office of Development, are systematically mobilizing the rich stewardship resources of the Church and making them available to us in a manner never accomplished before.

In my own diocese, we are learning more and more about the stewardship of money, and this learning is representative to some extent of what is emerging in various places throughout the Church. I would like to deal in depth with some of these learnings, and then conclude with a note about the future.

A recurring issue in the stewardship of money is whether a responsible giver results from a program of evangelism leading to a deeper or renewed commitment to Jesus as Lord, or from a thorough and systematic program of stewardship education. The answer we have found is that it is not an either/or matter. Both approaches can and do produce responsible giving in the Church, and therefore, neither should be regarded as the exclusive way. Sometimes it requires both for a given individual. Often it depends upon the make up of a parish and its priest, as well as its own history and how it views itself and the world at the given moment.

One of the key elements in our concept of stewardship is found in the word itself. A steward is literally one who manages or cares for another's property, money, or affairs. Implicit in this is the fact that *all* that the steward has comes from his master, that he literally owns nothing. All that he has or ever will have belongs to his master. Translated, this means an acknowledgement on the part of the individual believer that all that he possesses comes from God and still belongs to God. Until such an acknowledgement sinks deep into the heart and being, one should expect little growth in terms of personal stewardship.

If we believe that what we possess comes from us and belongs to us, then we will manage those possessions according to our own human values and not according to God's. Our own innate selfishness will dictate their use.

If, on the other hand, we acknowledge that all of our possessions come from God, what then? Where can we start in making God's value system our own? By seriously and prayerfully considering the tithe as the standard or norm—not as a law, but as a norm.

The notion of the tithe arose in the Old Testament and became a law for the Israelites. But notice the context of the first mention of a tithe. It is found in Genesis 28:22. It is Jacob's response to God for the magnificent dream God had given him at Bethel wherein God had promised to bless him and all his descendants and to give them the land they sought. Not because it was a law or a duty, but out of a deeply grateful heart Jacob responded to God "of all that Thou givest me I will give the tenth to thee." This was a free, unsolicited response of a grateful person to a loving God.

The tithe did not pass into the Christian tradition as law, but it did come to be accepted as a norm, a place where one could at least begin to live the life of a responsible steward. Jesus exposed the fallacy of all such laws and sought a free, spontaneous giving of the total person.

Seen as a norm, the tithe can be a beginning guide that opens the believer to respond in gratitude to a loving God. It is, furthermore, a gracious norm. God could easily have placed upon us a law of ninety percent. From the experience in our own diocese and other areas where we have worked, the tithe as a norm for Christian giving is essential to any sound program of stewardship education. This is further authenticated by the action of the House of Bishops and the Lambeth Conference, which are both on record as endorsing the tithe as a norm for Christian giving.

Undergirding this is the basic biblical and theological rationale for Christian giving—namely, we believe that Jesus died for us, just as we are, and that this dying took away the finality of death and gave us the assurance of eternal life. One way of expressing my deep gratitude and thankfulness to him for what he has done for me is to share with his Church and other people at least a portion of all that he has placed in my possession. Stripped to its essence, this is the only rationale for Christian giving and the only one worthy of Christian teaching. Some day we may be bold enough to proclaim this in its absolute purity!

In this whole process of stewardship education, we are beginning to learn more about what happens to people when they brush up against such teaching. Every person connected with the Church, no matter how vaguely, is often confronted with the matter of stewardship. How he or she deals with this confrontation affects radically their relationship to the Church. Seldom does anyone ever deal with this issue unemotionally, and experience has taught us that the issues usually shape up in one or more of the following ways:

"I would like to become a tither, but I get all tangled up in uncertainty about my financial ability, put off a decision and continue to feel badly about the whole matter."

"When I am asked to tithe I sometimes feel like I ought to, but then I feel silly because I don't really believe the tithe applies to me, and fear of being a sucker keeps me from acting."

"I feel like I ought to tithe, but I also get angry at the Church and don't really believe that my money does glorify God at all, so I do nothing and usually feel a little guilty."

These are just some of the ways to describe the shape of the issues where stewardship is concerned. The point is that this issue always seems to shape up around the dilemma, the uncertainty, the pain and agony of making a decision. Anxiety increases even more by the reality that there is potentially both cost and promise connected with any decision that we make. The uncertainty is in whether or not the price to be paid is too high. Usually the potential costs of accepting the tithe as a norm are more obvious. Some potential costs and potential promises may appear as fallacies:

SOME POTENTIAL COSTS

——If I become a tither, I may have to give up some things that I would really like to have.
——Tithing may actually impose a financial hardship upon me and my family.
——I will be unable to control in every instance how my money is used.
——A portion of my money may well be spent in ways not glorifying God, and in support of things that I abhor.
——I will be seen as a sucker in the eyes of some of my friends.
——I may discover that there is no blessedness at all in giving.

SOME POTENTIAL PROMISES

——I may discover that *things* in my life are less important than I thought.
——I may discover that a new attitude toward stewardship brings about new attitudes in how I manage the remainder of my resources.
——I may discover that my commitment decision about stewardship has some-

thing to do with my commitment to Jesus as Lord; and thus I may see considerable change brought about in my life.

—— I may discover that my commitment decision about stewardship has dealt with a great deal of guilt that I have felt about the matter, and, also, that some of my concern about how my money is spent has lessened in importance.

—— I may discover that with my decision tithing became *what is* a part of my life and not *what ought* to be, and that I will feel less defensive about the whole matter.

—— I may discover that there really is a blessedness in giving out of love.

Ultimately, everyone makes some kind of decision about stewardship. He may decide not to make a decision, he may decide not to become a tither, he may decide to become a tither or to work consistently and systematically toward that goal. The fact is that neither the potential costs nor the potential promises can become realities until some meaningful decision has been made.

At any rate, real decisions about stewardship are hard to make—they are very disturbing at the deepest level. Such decisions require that we stand naked before the Lord, stripped of all excuses, rationalizations, fantasies, and that we say to the Lord, "Here I am, I return what is yours." If you have not known the pain of that kind of decision, followed by the joyous freedom that comes with such a decision, it probably means that you have not yet made a realistic decision about your own personal stewardship of money.

Good stewardship education recognizes that it asks people to make hard decisions about their stewardship. It recognizes that those kinds of decisions are seldom made in a climate of coercion, but that they can be made in a climate where there is example, support, understanding, and some demonstrable realization that the decision is worth making. The process moves forward when there is an indication that the leadership of this education speaks either from the reality of its life, or is willing to take the first step into the unknown along with its people.

Here in the Diocese of Alabama, our own experience using this stewardship education program over the last seven years (referred to by those outside as "the Alabama Plan") has proven to us the reality of these principles and concepts. On the tangible, measurable side we have seen dramatic increases in individual giving, to the point of having the highest per capita giving among all the dioceses of the Episcopal Church. Inevitably, we see such other signs of renewal as the emergence of new and effective lay leadership, increased participation in the worship life of the parish, and a renewed sense of mission to the community.

At the heart of this stewardship education program is a set of eight criteria that the rector and vestry must "buy into" before the program will be instituted. They are not sacrosanct, but experience tells us that where they are compromised the program loses most, if not all, of its effectiveness. On the other hand, we know that they can be adapted to any size or type of parish in the Church. The criteria for entering into the stewardship education program are as follows:

1. *The rector is a tither or is committed to a personal program of proportionate giving, the minimum goal of which is tithing.* In other words, if the core and heart of the parish leadership is not committed, there is little or no chance of effective stewardship occurring.

2. *The vestry is officially committed to proportionate giving, the minimum goal of which is tithing, as the pattern for Christian stewardship, and shows this commitment by waiting until after the canvass to formulate its budget for the coming year.* By delaying the formulation of the budget, the educational process is focused on the growth and nurture of the individual's concept of stewardship and not on "raising a budget."

3. *The vestry is committed to a goal of giving $1.00 for work outside the parish for every $1.00 spent on itself.* This may seem overwhelming at first glance, but for most parishes it is a realistic, attainable goal. No time limit is set, but the vestry is asked to draw a plan with a time-line into the future, indicating the steps leading to the goal.

4. *Individual members of the vestry are committed to proportionate giving, the minimum goal of which is tithing, as the pattern of their own stewardship.* The leadership principle is the same as in point 1.

5. *Every member of the parish will be contacted by a trained canvasser in a direct, personal visit.* the trained, committed canvasser has some good news to share, and evey person in the parish has the right to hear it.

6. *One person for each four families in the parish will be recruited to participate in six hours of training, at the conclusion of which he may commit himself to serve as a canvasser.* Notice that only after the training are people asked to decide whether or not they would be canvassers. Only the committed person is an effective canvasser.

7. *The vestry commits itself to a systematic follow-up program (over a two-year period), using the assistance of a stewardship consultant.*

8. *The vestry agrees to pay a fee for the services of the stewardship consultant, plus providing his travel and lodging expenses for the number of days agreed to in writing after the exploratory meeting.* The amount of the fee is not important. What is important is that the parish make some investment of its own funds into the program to heighten its own sense of responsibility for success.

In terms of the future, there are increasing signs that there is an ever broadening and deepening sense of stewardship within the Church. The renewed sense of stewardship that is beginning to grow in this area is also beginning to grow in other areas. The emphasis of this stewardship is not upon meeting a budget (parish, diocese, or national) but on providing individuals with the opportunity to understand and respond to what the Lord Jesus has done and is doing for and with them. Budgets tend to be limited and restrictive, blurring our vision and restraining our horizon, but giving in a grateful response to what God has done for us knows no limit.

The Presiding Bishop has taken a strong step in this direction on the National Church level by advocating a departure from the one budget system whereby all giving to this level is funneled into one narrow conduit. In addition to the rather restrictive track we have known for some time, he envisions myriad ways that the people of this Church can express their response to God. It will not be just a matter of the individual giving to the parish, the parish to the diocese, and the diocese to the National Church. We will also see giving from individual to individual, parish to parish, diocese to diocese, individual to National Church, parish to National Church. This will have the effect of releasing more financial resources and opening up the Church more fully at all levels to mission and ministry.

Another hopeful sign for the future is the fact that the Church is beginning to articulate more clearly and effectively the needs of mission. The person who has made a responsible decision about stewardship will give, but he is more apt to do this for those needs that are clearly stated.

At a deeper level, the most hopeful sign for the future is the ever-increasing emphasis upon the theological and biblical rationale for the stewardship of giving. In the long haul, it is only this rationale that will sustain giving. And it will also provide the vital impetus to increase and multiply giving. St. Paul put it so well when he said, "Yet the proof of God's amazing love is this: that it was while we were yet sinners that Christ died for us" (Romans 5:6). There is an ever-increasing realization of this fact which augurs well for the corporate and individual state of stewardship in the Church at the moment and in the days to come.

PART II

Renewal, Evangelism, Education for Ministry

chapter 7

CONTEMPORARY SPIRITUALITY: SOME STRUCTURES AND STYLES

Dolores R. Leckey

INTRODUCTION

In his first letter to the Corinthians, Paul describes the Church as a body with different functions, and as the recipient of a variety of spiritual gifts, all related to its many functions (I Cor. 12). Throughout its history, the body has experienced fatigue and illness as well as élan vital (Bergson's term). The present moment is probably one of élan vital, a time of spiritual renaissance. And yet, I feel a certain hesitancy about using terms like *spirituality* or *spiritual development* in a discussion of the Church's contemporary and future experience. There are several reasons.

First, there are the misassociations which persist. Spiritual persons, it is assumed, are somehow set apart, either by vow (as in the case of monks and nuns), or by temperament and circumstances. In any case, they are different from and better than ordinary mortals. Spirituality is "out there" and does not readily mingle with flesh and blood and the routine of daily living—so it is said. Unfortunately, this image perdures despite the centrality of the Eucharist in our worship, which continually enacts the mingling of spirit and flesh, and despite our Johannine theology, which insists that "if we say we have no sin in us, we are deceiving ourselves and refusing to admit the truth" (I John 8).

I am hesitant for another reason. Spirituality is "in." Courses, retreats, and conferences on the subject are everywhere. The fastest moving books in the libraries are those on the occult and related psychic wonders. Furthermore, a whole new wave of meditators, encouraged by scientific interest and research, is practicing the ancient art for a variety of reasons: higher productivity, lower blood pressure, improved interpersonal relations. These are worthy reasons, certainly; but it can be difficult to distinguish fashionable spirituality from the arduous process of union with God. It might be well to heed the warning of the anonymous author of *The Cloud of the Unknowing*, that whenever an individual undertakes to bring his life into relation to God, he is embarking upon a serious and demanding task, a task that leaves no leeway for self-deception or illusion, but which requires the most rigorous dedication and self-knowledge.[1]

Lastly, something akin to fear of the Lord makes me hesitate. How does one dare to try to express what, in the final analysis, must be inexpressible? One dares, I think, because of the conviction that John Dunne is right, that "communicating whatever limited insight one has found might in fact be the best method of searching for the way."[2]

SPIRITUALITY AS PILGRIMAGE

The Second Vatican Council declared that the Church is primarily a pilgrim people.[3] It was a phrase with which most of the Christian Churches could identify; it spoke to the heart of Christian experience.

This experience is portrayed most graphically for me in William Blake's engraving, *The Canterbury Pilgrims*. Chaucer's characters are all there, from the wife of Bath to the youthful Abbess; from the shipman to the Oxford scholar. They are depicted in the dynamic Blake manner, all movement and life and energy. The company is leaving Tabarde Inn, and they are pierced by the first rays of morning. Standing at the gateway are an old man, a woman, and some children. It is a visual microcosm, and a powerful image for what I will call spirituality. This spirituality encompasses all kinds of people from all walks of life who share fully and equally in the holy adventure of this pilgrimage. When their stories are told and their personal revelations shared, all are listened to with equal respect and attention. It is a model, I believe, for spiritual movements in the Church.

Just as the medieval pilgrimage was an event outside the habitual Church structures, so the movements, which I will call spiritual pilgrimages, are noticeably on the edges of congregational and parish life. They are not outside the life of the Church (as the pilgrimage was not outside the Church), but removed from the ordinary, organizational life of the Church.

What follows are reflections on some of these pilgrimages, the reflections of a Roman Catholic pilgrim who has been and is part of them. There are some projections, too, for what they might mean for an evolving Church—tomorrow's Church of grace.

SOLITUDE AND INTIMACY

One pilgrimage characteristic in particular has the potential for a profound impact on the future mission of the Church; it is that solitude and society are not antithetical in the pilgrimage event. Especially during the Middle Ages they were considered complementary modes of being; and to my mind they were analogous to God's mode of being. They are analogous, too, to authentic spiritual growth. For the movement of the individual spirit to a growing consciousness of God within and a growing love of all that God is, while intensely personal, is never exclusive. I think it was Dante who said that when a soul ceases to say "mine" and says "ours," it makes the transition from the narrow, constricted life to the truly free and creative spiritual life.

It has long been recognized that solitude is *the* essential for creativity. Inevitably, it leads one to questions of ultimate value, questions of life and death, good and evil, love and power. Solitude is also the pathway to concentration. It is necessary for learning to be attentive and for learning to love. People who are in love need time to simply *be* with each other; so do God and the human spirit. For love is the very substance of spirituality. Perhaps this is why William James has defined solitude as the primary condition for religious experience.[4]

With the exception of the eremitical vocation, solitude provides only a partial means for a healthy spiritual life. Intimate society is equally as important, for I think it is quite true that it is not being alone that people fear most, but being misunderstood.

We need to communicate with others the fruits of solitude and to bring these experiences into the light of community discernment. Apart from this, intimacy is in itself a place where dialogues of the heart and spirit may occur, and where the divine encounter can happen. These dialogues are a dynamic of giving, receiving, changing. They may be times of affirmation and communion, or of confrontation and struggle; but if they are truly dialogic, they will be energizing because of the truth spoken and shared and the freedom experienced.

These rhythms of solitude and intimate society don't just happen, even in explicitly religious gatherings. They are being discovered and lived into through inner journeying, spiritual pilgrimages into the realms of prayer.

SOME MODERN PILGRIMAGE ROUTES

The charismatic movement is by now one well-known dimension of the prayer pilgrimage. Interestingly enough, it is flourishing in Churches with rich sacramental and liturgical traditions—like the Episcopal and the

Roman Catholic. With its spontaneous style and flexible structures, the charismatic prayer meeting leads the worshipers to God through the unexpected. The immanence of God, rather than his transcendence, is the normative experience. Liturgy, with its context of symbols and ritual, leads the worshipers by way of the expected into a transcendent awareness of God. (Of course, theologians are careful to describe the divine as both immanent and transcendent.) The readiness of liturgical Christians to embrace the free-form, ecstatic style is an example, I think, of our striving for inclusiveness and balance, for a more complete encounter with the divine. We would be deterred from approximating the balance, however, if the charismatic prayer form were to be the only one in the life of the worshiper; or if liturgy, on the other hand, were to be the sole expression. This is one important consideration for the Church of tomorrow.

Charismatic prayer is well known because it is vocal and visible. There is relatively little known about another prayer pilgrimage, namely, the way of contemplative prayer, or the *prayer of quiet*. In the past, it was often thought to be the exclusive path for those chosen by God for mystic graces. However, it is now being explored by those who think it possible that Thomas Aquinas was right when he taught that contemplation is potentially proper to all, and that, indeed, it is the most thoroughly human activity.

There have always been some who have managed to pass unaided through discursive "mental" prayer to the contemplative prayer of quiet in the natural course of their development. But there have also been others who have longed to do so and did not know how. "Lord, teach us to pray" has been a muffled cry in many of our churches.

Now, however, with the ecumenical borders between the Christian West and the great religions of the East opened, and with dialogue and spiritual intercourse a reality, we have been put in touch with skillful means for entering more directly into the center of contemplative silence. It is not unusual to find dedicated and wholly committed Christians engaged in visualizations, chanting, mantras, and the like in order to develop open, receptive attitudes for prayer, the kind of prayer which Simone Weil spoke of as absolute attentiveness to God.

Quiet prayer pilgrimages are happening in both likely and unlikely places. Monasteries, whose *raison d'etre* has been contemplation and conscious union with God, are sharing their knowledge and experience through workshops and retreats—a kind of monastic outreach. The Metropolitan Ecumenical Training Center of Washington, D.C., with a history of working primarily in the social justice arena, could be considered an unlikely medium; yet, it conducts long-term meditation and spiritual development groups, which are open to clergy and laity.

Contact with Eastern religious practices has stimulated research into the Western mystical tradition in its many varieties, and into Eastern Orthodox spirituality. The Jesus Prayer,[5] for example, is very natural for Christian meditators and is becoming rather widely practiced. Another inheritance from Russia, the *poustinia*,[6] has only recently been introduced into Western spiritual practice and is still relatively unknown.

The Cursillo movement[7] has addressed itself to the need for intimate community in a fairly structured way. Following the Cursillo weekend, arrangements are made for small groups, stable in membership, to meet once a week. Four or five persons come together for the purpose of a continuing experimental awareness of Christ. It is a place of accountability in terms of developing spiritual disciplines and life styles consistent with the Gospel imperatives. Beyond the accountability aspect, these meetings are often described as Emmaus-like, when through existential revelation, the Word is once again made flesh.

MUTUALITY: RELATING CHURCH AND PILGRIMAGE

What is the appropriate relationship and the appropriate spheres of influence between the Church and the contemporary spiritual pilgrimage? Victor Turner speaks of the *survival* of the pilgrimage occurring when it imparts to religious orthodoxy a renewed vitality, rather than when it asserts against an established system a set of heterodox opinions and unprecedented styles of religious and symbolic action.[8] Most often, the medieval pilgrim was not concerned about institutionalizing the sacred journey. It was experienced as a flowing event, and it led one eventually back home to stability and institution. For the Church's part, it recognized and allowed the pilgrimage to be elastically related to it. The returned pilgrim's presence, however, did change the institutional equation in subtle but very real ways. Wisdom and enlightenment make a gentle impact.

At this writing, I feel confident that the spiritual renaissance will reach into the depths of the institutional Church. This stance of hope is based on the fact that so many clergy and lay leaders are themselves on spiritual pilgrimage of one kind or another. Because of this, I think it possible that the local churches—and the Church at large—will not view the places of prayer and community which lie outside the parish as a judgment on it or in competition with it. I realize that development of these attitudes will call for large portions of humility from both pilgrim and local church. (Here humility is meant as St. Therese of Liseaux defined it: openness to the truth.)

What, precisely, can the returning pilgrim offer to the Church? First, like his medieval counterpart, he can offer *presence*. He can be available to share the experience of spiritual pilgrimage: the ways of meditation, silence, prayer, and personal dialogue. Others may be encouraged, through this sharing, to venture forth.

Then, too, the pilgrim's presence at corporate worship is likely to be enthusiastic; he will be acquainted with openness and a heightened awareness.

If the priest happens to be the pilgrim, he becomes a gateway for many others. It is very possible that he will have developed a charism for spiritual direction, a gift very much needed in the Church. Unlike counseling, where one is working toward freedom to act, spiritual direction assumes realization of one's freedom. The issue becomes the use of that freedom for the love of God and neighbor. Spiritual direction moves one beyond the conventional responses to the radical *Yes* of the Gospel. For the pilgrim/priest/spiritual director to become a reality, congregations will have to give their priests the gift of time, and opportunities for solitude and intimate society.

This gift to the priest might be the first gesture or model for honoring the rhythms of solitude and intimate society in the lives of other members of the parish. This will mean that tomorrow's Church, instead of pointing members toward organizations to join and projects to undertake, would provide them with space—psychic space as well as floor space—in order to develop their contemplative capacities. I am not here advocating a return to sixteenth-century quietism. The authentic inner spiritual experience has always been marked by an outward thrust, as demonstrated in the lives of mystics of all traditions. The key is allowing the action to unfold, for the action is simply the spiritual experience made visible.

If the future Church takes this seriously, it will find itself less concerned with using people's time and energy for its own upbuilding and organizational maintenance, and more concerned with freeing and empowering its members to be faithful to their vocations in the world, and to *be* there in the world as personal centers of peace and understanding.

The most important gift, I believe, which the Church can offer the pilgrim is a sense of lineage. This is realized in the following ways: (1) Group consciousness, chiefly through liturgy and creed; (2) Religious union, not only with contemporaries but extending into the past, a union with the race and with history; (3) Discipline, which corrects subjectivity (extremely important for pilgrims who may be steeped in an unfocused, indiscriminate enthusiasm); (4) Culture, that is, a handing on of the wisdom of the saints.[9] I would like to suggest that this stability and rootedness is probably quite enough for any parish—which is the concrete expression of the Church—to extend to its members. I am beginning to feel that we have expected too much of the parish, and too many of the wrong things. Such unreal expectations can overshadow the real spiritual mission of the Church.

If there are fewer tasks to be accomplished in tomorrow's Church, perhaps there will be more encouragement of the dialogues of the heart. This is first and foremost to be found in spiritual direction. It should not be assumed, however, that this charism is automatically resident with the priest, even if he is a pilgrim priest. This particular gift is characterized by qualities of empathy, humility, clarity of mind, generosity of spirit, and discernment. Since good directors usually do not advertise, preferring to be "hidden away with Christ in God" (Col. 3:3), finding a director is often a problem. It will be incumbent upon ecclesiastical authorities, therefore, to be alert for those priests and laity who are persons of prayer, those who have perhaps been on pilgrimage, who have discerning wisdom, who are knowledgeable about the Church's indissoluble relationship with Christ, and who are willing to enter into the intense interpersonal relationship of spiritual direction. It is not likely, even if attention is given to the development of directors, that their numbers will be great. But the Church can also facilitate small groups, as in the Cursillo, for purposes of spiritual growth. We have Christ's promise to be present in these gatherings. If the Church can diffuse the subtle pressures to "produce results," many benefits of spiritual direction can be felt.

Furthermore, dialogues of the heart inevitably must consider the value of men and women in relationship as well as what this means for individual spiritual growth, the development of the Church as a whole, and the spiritual maturation of society. Beyond the fundamental apprehension of the masculine/feminine relationship as co-equal, interdependent, and complementary, there are the more programmatic implications of this for our patterns of marriage, work, and worship.[10] I think the Church must promote theological and personal reflection on the spiritual realities underlying human sexuality, and promote this on the parish level. The theology of marriage as continuing sacramental encounter has been sadly neglected; filial love and friendship, so vital in the life of Jesus, deserve to be explored; and celibacy as a life-style should be pondered. The spiritual power of our sexuality is still to be tapped.

It should be evident by now that I hope and expect the Church of tomorrow to encourage and rejoice in spiritual pilgrimages. But there is another phenomenon I feel sure must happen to some degree, and it will also affect the Church.

The Middle Ages was the age of pilgrimage and it was also the age of orders. Religious communities sprang up all over Europe, often as the result of a pilgrimage. It was a case of having been so radically touched by the sacred event, that an ideal Gospel life-style was attempted to preserve the integrity of the original experience. This was seen as healthy for the Church, a sign of God's blessing. It was also acknowledged that not everyone was so touched.

In a similar vein, I sense a growing tendency on the part of some spiritual pilgrims to form extracongregational communities with a degree of permanence. Already there are households and residential communities connected with the charismatic movement, with liberation theology and commitment to the poor. My intuition is that religious associations or contemporary third orders[11] are on the horizon. Long-term spiritual development groups, workshops, and retreats have been a form of apprenticeship or postulancy. But there will be in the future, as there was in the past, a need for places where one can live out more fully and deeply the insights of spiritual pilgrimage.

Like Blake's engraving, the pilgrimages I have been discussing have a rich mixture of people from varied backgrounds. In many ways, these pilgrimages are experiences beyond ecumenism as we have been accustomed to think of it. Denominational lines are not crossed so much as transcended, and the unity which is the *reality* at the core of life is felt and affirmed. My hope, and it is a hope joined with faith, is that the Church—larger than any parish or diocese or denomination—the Church of Christ Our Lord will listen with care to the new stories (which are really old stories) that pilgrims have to tell about life at the center, about how the Lord is one and we are one. I even hope—and believe—that the Church will act upon what is heard, moving us all closer to the Omega point.

NOTES

1. *The Cloud of the Unknowing*, trans. Ira Progoff (New York: Delta Publishing Co., 1957), p. 19.

2. John S. Dunne, *The Way Of All The Earth* (New York: Macmillan Publishing Co., 1972), p. 39.

3. The Church as pilgrim is a theme to be found in most of the Vatican Council II documents. It is pronounced, however, in the *Dogmatic Constitution on the Church*.

4. James's definition of religious experience as quoted by Evelyn Underhill is as follows: "The feelings, acts and experiences of individuals in their solitude so far as they apprehend themselves to stand in relation to whatever they consider Divine." *The Evelyn Underhill Reader,* Thomas Kepler, ed. (New York: Abingdon Press, 1962), p. 218.

5. The basic text of the Jesus Prayer is: "Lord Jesus Christ, Son of God, have mercy upon me a sinner." It is usually prayed in coordination with one's breathing. There is a growing body of literature around the prayer.

6. The word *poustinia* means desert in Russian. It refers to a Russian hermitage experience. In spiritual practice it consists of a stark, bare room, with a board bed (or no bed), a large wooden cross without a corpus, a Bible and perhaps a writing table and a straight back chair. For twenty-four hours your only food is bread, your only drink water, your only reading the Scriptures. You are in a desert,

awaiting the revelation of God. The history and practice is fully explained in Catherine deHueck Doherty, *Poustinia* (Notre Dame, Indiana: Ave Maria Press, 1975).

7. The Cursillo is a weekend experience in intense Christian community. Through lectures, sharing, liturgy, prayer and penance, Christ in oneself and in the other person is revealed. The movement originated in Spain and the word literally means a short course in Christianity.

8. Victor Turner, *Dramas, Fields, and Metaphors* (Ithaca and London: Cornell University Press, 1974), p. 227.

9. *The Evelyn Underhill Reader*, p. 219.

10. These terms are Dr. William Davidson's, a psychiatrist, who is publishing a book on the male-female diad and its significance for world order.

11. Third Orders arose in the thirteenth century out of the mendicant orders, Franciscans and Dominican. Friars were the First Order, nuns formed the Second Order, and lay people the Third Order. They spread rapidly throughout Europe, embracing multitudes of men and women of all ranks from highest to lowest. Some lived together in community and some lived in the world. All lived under a rule of life.

chapter 8

EVANGELISM IN THE CHURCH: AN OVERVIEW*

O.C. Edwards, Jr.

I am deeply committed to the necessity for the Church to evangelize, but I have grave reservations about the Episcopal Church's modeling its evangelistic techniques too closely after those of revivalism, Fundamentalism, and conservative evangelical Protestantism. My reason for having such reservations are that McLuhan's point that the medium is the message seems to be especially accurate in relation to the Gospel message. This is to say that evangelical methods often give unrealistic notions about what the Episcopal Church is like, so that our converts could say that we bring them in under false pretenses. By the same token, these techniques fail to emphasize the real glories of our tradition, the blessings we have that we should be most willing to share with others.

This point is closely allied with another: that we have fallen into language habits by which we have come to think of evangelism exclusively in terms of what evangelists in the evangelical tradition do, and have thus forgotten that the Church was an evangelistic movement for some seventeen centuries before these techniques began to be developed on the American frontier. As a matter of fact, evangelism has continued to be done all along by Episcopalians and others without employing those techniques at all. Thus, if we are supposed to do evangelism, it is a great mistake to think that we have to do what those in the evangelical tradition do.

All evangelism, of course, grows out of personal witness and testimony. In this paper, therefore, I will begin with my own conversion narrative and then try to use some insights of learning theory and the sociology of knowledge to analyze what it is that we do when we engage in evangelism. With that analysis in mind, I will then do a historical survey of evan-

---

*This article appears in the special General Convention issue of the *Anglican Theological Review*.

gelism. It will, of course, be impossible to be anything but highly selective in the historical phenomena at which we look, so I will choose three periods that help us to distinguish between several kinds of activity that often get lumped together as evangelism. On the basis of that I will discuss the nature of the evangelistic task before the Episcopal Church today and the methods that are consistent with and effective for that task.

I should say at once that I will be discussing not my conversion to Christianity but my conversion to the Episcopal Church. I grew up in a Christian home and I do not remember when I have not believed myself to be a Christian or when I was not happy with the idea of being one. I grew up in a small town that is in the geographical center of North Louisiana. Except for a few Jewish merchants and their families and an Italian shoe repairman, I believe that everyone in that town was a Protestant Christian; although some were good Christians and some were bad. And their Christianity was of a particular sort. Southern Baptists were most numerous, Methodists came next, and then the Nazarenes. There were several small congregations of holiness sects of one kind or another. Blacks did not worship in the same churches as whites, but the theologies taught in both were very similar. There were no Episcopalians in town, nor, for that matter, any Presbyterians or Lutherans. This is to say that the major traditions of the Reformation were absent. We knew nothing but the religion of the American frontier: revivalist, Fundamentalist, evangelical Protestantism. Even the town's most notorious sinners shared the same view of reality that all their neighbors did.

Let me summarize what we all believed: Every word in the Bible is literally, historically true. The Bible tells of the omnipotent God who created the world and everything in it in a calendar week of seven twenty-four-hour days. The first man and woman, Adam and Eve, disobeyed him and were cast from the bliss of the Garden of Eden, and all of their descendants have suffered from their fall. All men are sinners in need of a redeemer. Their sins consist generally in breaking the Ten Commandments and, more specifically, of smoking, drinking, playing cards (whether for money or not), dancing, mixed bathing, cursing; and in breaking the Sabbath by fishing, hunting, working, or going to the movies. God hates sin and he punishes those who commit it by sending them to hell when they die—a literally burning hell. He has provided an escape from hell by sending his Son Jesus to die for sinners. Those who will accept Jesus as their personal Savior undergo a conversion experience marked by intense emotion.

The major point of theological difference in our town was whether a person once in grace through conversion is always in grace or whether he is capable of "backsliding." Those who do persevere prove that they have been saved by avoiding the sins that we have listed and by attending church twice and Sunday School once every Sunday, prayer meeting every Wednesday night, and by reading their Bibles and praying daily in between. They also attend revival meetings that are held annually (usually the second week in August). When they die they are taken up immediately into heaven which they enter through pearly gates and then they spend eternity among the streets of gold.

Let me assure you that I have no desire to caricature or patronize that point of view, nor do I wish to imply that it is all bad by any means. Much about the system was good. Much about our town was very good, and most of my childhood memories are very pleasant. But I was converted away from that point of view to an Anglican understanding of Christianity, and I think the reasons why are still valid. The beginning of that conversion must go back to my early teens when my family moved from that small town to the comparatively large city of Shreveport. Although most of the people I met in our section of Shreveport in those days had much the same worldview that I had known before, there were significant exceptions. I was confronted with cultural pluralism for the first time. I discovered that there were people who understood the universe differently from the way everyone I had known previously had understood it. What is more, as time went on I came to see that some of the interpretations that other people made appeared to make more sense and to account more adequately for all the data of my own experience than what I had been brought up to believe.

This process was spread out over a number of years and was not completed until I was a senior in a Methodist seminary. I can, however, point to three areas in which my faith was tried. The first of these was theological. I came to doubt the literal inerrancy of the Bible. Where I was brought up, evolution was believed to be a doctrine of the devil. I can still remember vividly when I accidentally opened a zoology textbook to the page on which was printed a chart showing the skeletons of the major groups of vertebrates. From that moment on I could not doubt evolution, and I could not believe in the literal historicity of the early chapters of Genesis. And that was not all. The doctrine of inerrancy had made the authority of the Bible an all-or-nothing proposition. If you could not believe every word of it, what reliance could you put in any of it? Finally, at the seminary I came under the disturbing influence of the then prevalent theological liberalism that saw no special place for Jesus in Theology beyond being a religious genius, a great teacher and example.

The second area in which my faith was challenged was in the area of morals. I came to know people who committed what I had been taught to regard as sins and who had no compunction about it. Nor, as far as that goes, could I see that they were less attractive as human beings than the people who disapproved of those things. Often, in fact, the contrary was true. And, to tell the truth, I came to experiment with some of the milder of these things myself and could not honestly believe that I was the worse for doing so. As a matter of fact, much of what I had been taught was sinful came to appear very trivial and it became hard for me to take seriously anyone who took such things seriously. At the same time, I was being alerted to what did appear to me to be serious moral issues—war, race relations, and the like—and I noticed that the people who made so much fuss about the things that I had come to regard as just silly were absolutely untroubled by the moral problems that occupied my thoughts.

The third area in which I discovered that my own opinions had begun to diverge from those of the community in which I had been brought up was in my thoughts about religious experience. I had been taught that what makes one a Christian was a dramatic conversion experience, and that anyone who could not tell you the day and the hour of his conversion was still a lost sinner who was bound for hell. While there are only a few occasions when the Methodists I knew shouted or were taken with any of the more picturesque forms of behavior, the altar call was made not only during the annual revival meetings, but as the closing part of most regular services. While we could not count on a supply of the unsaved to be present on all such occasions, we could at least expect that there would be someone there who needed to rededicate his life to God. The sawdust trail was also open to that kind of traffic and the visible emotional manifestations were not markedly different. (Nothing was more obvious than who had religious experiences and what the intensity and frequency of them were.) Thus one could hardly avoid the observation that there was no discernible connection between the dramatic quality of the experience and the attractiveness of the life of the person who had it. As the people in the congregation whom I respected least were those whose experiences seemed most regular and intense, experience came to appear to me to be the least reliable criterion for evaluating someone's religion.

So far all of this has been negative, and shows only how I was "converted away" from the religion of my childhood. We can now move to the positive side—my conversion to the Episcopal Church. The first step came far ahead of the others and became "a treasure in the field" that lay forgotten for a long time until I happened to be in the vicinity again and thought to unearth it. One of my best friends in college was an Episcopalian and he invited me to attend Midnight Mass with him on Christmas. I went out of a combination of curiosity, a wish to scoff, and the desire to have something to do. That night I discovered the beauty of holiness or the holiness of beauty or whatever it should be called. I will never forget the impact of the candles and the vestments and that glorious solemn language. I had no intellectual categories by which I could interpret what I saw as religious, but this new vision of the possibilities of beauty was breathtaking and that vision is one I have never been able to forget.

The next step in my conversion came when I was a Methodist seminarian. My professor of theology was deeply influenced by the Neo-orthodox movement that was so conspicuous a part of the theological scene at the time, and he was a brilliant and profound thinker. He quickly demonstrated to us the superficiality of the old-school liberalism that most of us, without having thought the matter through in any very thorough manner, had come to accept as the enlightened view of religion. We had assumed that evolution implied inevitable progress in society, that mankind was moving ever onward and upward toward perfection, and that we did not have much further to go. He showed us that two world wars in a quarter of a century, the most brutal the world had ever known—and both of them started by the technologically most advanced nation of the world—gave little support to an optimistic view of man.

Individual men and mankind in general are hopelessly self-centered and that selfishness spoils even their noblest acts. Man is a sinner and he is incapable of doing anything good without the assistance of God. Man is a sinner in need of a redeemer. This low anthropology calls for a high Christology. Classical Christian orthodoxy does not depend on biblical literalism. We all became quite fond of saying with Reinhold Niebuhr that the myths of the Bible did not have to be taken literally, but they did have to be taken seriously. While Genesis does not teach us accurate astronomy, geology, or history, it does teach us religion that is a great deal more accurate and adequate than our pseudosophistication.

My attraction to classical orthodoxy, however, posed an additional problem for me. My tutors in liberalism had been clergy. How was it that the official spokesmen of a Christian body had led me into opinions that were un-Christian in the most literal sense possible? Because they had no place for Christ? In time my answer to that question became a historical answer. On the frontier, American Christianity had lost its continuity with historic Christianity, and had thus lost its criteria and safeguards. The only denominations that had escaped both Fundamentalism and liberalism were those that had historical continuity with the Church through the ages. These denominations included, most notably, the Roman Catholics, the Lutherans, and the Episcopalians. Habit was too strong for me to think seriously about Roman Catholicism, and Lutheranism was not around in enough force to be investigated. So I began to look at the Episcopal Church. Its principle of apostolic succession seemed to furnish the principle of historic continuity that could furnish the safeguard of orthodoxy for which I looked. I was confirmed in the Episcopal Church, and shortly afterwards I was transferred to an Episcopal seminary.

The process of religious naturalization and acculturation was far more complex than anything that could be fully described here, but I do want to tell you what it felt like. I felt like Hans Christian Anderson's "ugly duckling" when he discovered that he was really a swan. I felt like Willie Morris did when he realized that he had gone *North Toward Home.* After what had seemed like a lifetime in which my reflexes and reactions had been inappropriate for the society in which I lived, and after feeling left out and peculiar, I found a world in which my reflexes seemed normal. I felt that I had experienced a second birth, this time into a world in which I fit and to which I belonged. I felt right at home and have felt that way ever since. This was my conversion. It did mean new life to me, and my life has ever since been lived in gratitude to God for giving it to me.

Now I would like to move on to an analysis of what is involved, not only in that one conversion but in all conversions. The first studies of conversion were made by the psychologists of religion from the turn of the present century through its first quarter. They saw that the one general feature all conversions involved was "a change from an unorganized life to a life organized around a central idea" (A.C. Bouquet, "Conversion," *Encyclopaedia Britannica,* 14th ed., VI, 353). What this definition does not deal with in an adequate way is *how* life gets organized around a central idea and, even more, how that central idea can be replaced.

Contemporary learning theory, drawing from the work of Piaget and others, points out that we are constantly bombarded with sensations. Our senses have infinitely more impressions than they can process. We have a sensory overload and our mind deals with it by doing an immense amount of sorting. Sensations are fitted into categories of experience, and only those categories of sensations that have been designated as significant ever emerge into consciousness. One important implication of this is that our consciousness never encounters external reality immediately and directly. As aware as we are of seeing, hearing, tasting, smelling, and touching, the overwhelming majority of our sensations never get to our conscious awareness because they are filtered out by this sorting process long before they get that far. Thus, even in our clearest feeling of being in touch with the world around us, we never encounter it as it is in itself, but we always encounter only those aspects of it that our mind has selected out as being important for us.

The next thing we need to notice about all this is that the mind does not just sort sensations into categories but rates the categories for their relative importance. Trivial and irrelevant sensations are not selected for conscious awareness. Not only that, the categories exist in a hierarchy of progressively greater inclusiveness, so that the sorting apparatus of the mind involves a picture of the universe as a whole. In order for this whole machinery for dealing with our sensory overload to operate, we have to have something like a metaphysic: we have to have an understanding of the nature of ultimate reality. This need, which Clement Welsh has described as "a strain toward ultimates," is not something that is peculiar to man; scientists have shown that even one-cell organisms must in some sense "know" their environment.

Of course, this need to know what the universe is like is closely related to religion. Our beliefs about God are our ultimately most inclusive categories for the interpretation of our experience. Now all of our categories are susceptible to modification. Piaget has pointed out that the mind is constantly at work, not only in assimilating our sensations to the categories we already have, but also in accommodating those categories so that they are more adequate to the variety of sensations we experience. Since, however, we depend on those categories for being able to cope with the flood of sensations we experience, the categories need to be as stable as possible, so the mind has great resistance to the necessity of accommodation. It only changes its categories when it is forced to do so. The more inclusive the category, the more resistant it is to change. Thus our fundamental ideas about the universe, such as our beliefs about God, are changed only under necessity and never without a sense of great threat to the personality.

The last point we need to make about the way fundamental thinking is done is that it would be impossible for the mind of one individual to devise sufficient categories into which it could sort all that individual's experiences. The great majority of these categories are borrowed from the social group of which one is a member. The society has been assimilating and accommodating for some time, and it has arrived corporately at a picture of the universe as a whole that is shared by all its members and passed on to all those who are born into it or enter it some other way. This picture of the universe that is shared by a social group is what the sociologists Peter Berger and Thomas Luckmann refer to as a "social construction of reality." Each new member of the society is socialized into that construction of reality, and the group is continually legitimating that construction by accommodating it to include all new experience that does not appear immediately to be consistent with it. Sometimes the categories are not elastic enough to accommodate all of the inconsistent data, and then that particular construction of reality collapses.

With such an analysis of the way fundamental thinking occurs, we are now in a position to see both how conversion, in general, can be the change from an unorganized life to a life organized around a central idea, and what, in particular, occurred in my conversion. This will then give us the tools to analyze what has happened in the way of evangelism throughout the course of Church history.

First, my conversion. I was brought up in a society that constructed reality in a certain way, that of revivalist-Fundamentalist evangelical Protestantism. My own efforts to legitimate that construction of reality into which I had been socialized became progressively more difficult for me until finally the construction as a whole collapsed as far as I was concerned. That is to say, I could no longer participate fully in the group that constructed reality that way. Now, the disconfirmatory evidence with which I was trying to cope was seen by me to be incorporated all along into the construction of reality held by other groups. When I finally settled on the Episcopal Church, I did so because its construction of reality was the one most consistent with the picture of the universe that my experience implied.

That construction has been more than adequate to every new need for legitimation that I have encountered since. This is to say that when a person is converted, he moves from membership in a group that constructs reality one way to a group that constructs it another way. Notice, then, that conversion is not an experience of an isolated individual, but is always the transition of an individual from one group to another. This transition is usually accompanied by strong emotions because of the resistance the mind makes to the accommodation of its fundamental categories, but the essential element of conversion is in the area of belief rather than in that of emotion. Life is organized around the central ideas of the new group.

The first period in the evangelistic history of the Church on which I would like us to focus attention is that which begins with the ministry of Jesus and lasts until A.D. 392, when the Roman Emperor Theodosius the Great forbade pagan worship under the same kind of penalties that Christian worship had been forbidden a century before. Thus, in a little over 350 years after the crucifixion, Christianity was the only legal religion in the Roman Empire; that is, in most of the civilized world. I think no one will question that this was a period of intense and successful evangelistic activity. As a matter of fact, we can see indications of how successful it was at a much earlier date. In the year A.D. 49, about fifteen years after we think the crucifixion must have been, the Emperor Claudius drove the Jews out of Rome. We are told that he did so because of the disturbances within the Jewish community at the instigation of a certain "Chrestus." It seems likely that this meant "Christus," and that Christianity was already so important in the capital of the Roman Empire that it had come to the unfavorable attention of the emperor. We know that fifteen years after that, when the Emperor Nero was suspected of setting the fire that destroyed Rome, he looked around for a bugbear on which he could shift the blame, an ancient Mediterranean equivalent of a red menace or a yellow peril. The Christians were already so known and feared that they seemed a natural choice. For this to have happened in the first Christian generation means that someone was spreading the word somewhere.

We should not fail to note the real differences between the evangelistic activity of Jesus and that of the early Church. The message of Jesus was that the kingdom of God was at hand, that God was intervening in history, bringing to an end the control of the forces of evil—the devil and his unclean spirits—over history, and inaugurating the control of the forces of good. Several characteristics of Jesus' mission call for attention. The first is that the crisis to which he called his audience to respond—that of the inbreaking of the reign of God—was occurring during his ministry. The people to whom his message was addressed were his co-religionists, the Jews. He himself was only incidentally the subject of his proclamation. What he proclaimed was the nearness of the reign of God, and his reference to himself was chiefly as the one through whose ministry it was being inaugurated. Finally, we need to notice about his mission that it was by and large unsuccessful in that instead of submitting to the yoke of the kingdom, his co-religionists rejected him and even executed him for blasphemy.

At this point I have just one observation: there is a technical term to describe the effort to persuade those who hold one doctrine, or who belong to one denomination within a religion, to accept another doctrine or denomination within that same religion and that term is "proselytism." The first evangelistic efforts of the primitive Church were proselytism; that is, they were also directed to the Jews. It was not until about A.D. 90 that it became clear to everyone that Christianity was more than just a sect within Judaism, distinguished from the rest of Judaism only by its belief that Jesus was the Messiah the Jews had long expected. Notice that the emphasis of their doctrine had already shifted from that of the message of Jesus; instead of the inbreaking reign of God, their major point was the Messiahship of Jesus. That, in fact, was implied by what Jesus said, but there is a difference. Their efforts to convert fellow Jews were no more successful than those of Jesus had been, and by the end of the Bar Kochba rebellion in A.D. 135, Jewish Christianity, for all practical purposes, could be said to have passed out of existence.

The first real missionary activity—the first efforts to convert those who belonged to entirely different religions—began much earlier. The gentile mission, as it is called, began around A.D. 50 and soon got its most powerful leadership from the apostle Paul. The message to the Greco-Roman world was very different than that to the Jews. The main point on which Jews needed to be persuaded was that the Messiah for whom they had been waiting had appeared as Jesus of Nazareth. The main point that needed to be made to the ancient peoples who lived around the Mediterranean was that there is only one God. This point had quickly to be followed by another, that this God expected ethical behavior from his people. They had no difficulty whatsoever in believing that there was a divine person; the hard thing was to convince them that there was *only* one.

One of the most surprising things for the modern Christian to learn about the Greco-Roman world into which the young Church moved is that there was virtually nothing comparable from which people could be converted to Christianity. Throughout the ancient world, with the notable exception of the Jews, religion was essentially a matter of state. A city-state or a kingdom had an alliance with a god or gods, by which the gods provided material prosperity and military success to the political body, and the body, in turn, saw that the things pleasing to the god—usually sacrifices and athletic competitions to entertain him—were provided for him. Religion, then, was much more a matter of politics than it was of piety. The average citizen was hardly involved, except as his taxes might have gone to pay for the sacrifices and games. About the time of Christ, there was an influx of new religions that were more individual and personal, but they consisted largely of undergoing initiatory rites in order to achieve immortality and health. There was nothing exclusive in the demands they made; one man could be initiated into several religions with no sense of inconsistency, just as one could believe in and worship all the gods of all the states. There was no further demand on the lives of those who adhered, nor were there communities of people who lived their lives in devotion to those gods and in an effort to carry out their principles.

The nearest analogy to Christianity in the ancient world was not another religion but philosophy. As Arthur Darby Nock has pointed out: (1) it offered an intelligible explanation of phenomena; (2) it offered life with a scheme, a discipline, and a goal; (3) it produced the saints of antiquity; (4) it had the influence of the living teacher; and (5) it made a literary appeal. One could be converted to philosophy as a total way and view of life, and one could be converted away from it to Christianity as a superior version of the same thing. (A. D. Nock, *Conversion.* New York: Oxford University Press, 1961., p. xi.)

The second period in Church history to which I would like to call attention began at about the time of the Reformation. Not all the areas of a country responded to the reforming movement in the same way. The southern part of Germany, for instance, remained loyal to the pope, while northern Germany went over to the side of Luther. The question of how it would be decided who belonged to which denomination arose. It was settled in the terms of the Peace of Augsburg in 1555 by the principle of *cujus regio ejus religio,* which is to say that the ruler of a region gets to pick the religion of the region. His subjects had no say in the matter. The Reformation in England has been described as largely a matter of state, but this is as true of Lutheranism and Calvinism as it was of Anglicanism to the extent that it was largely the political powers who decided if a territory would go over to the side of the Reformation or remain in communion with Rome.

Up until that time it had never occurred to anyone that you could have a realm that was united politically and yet divided religiously. It was largely due to England's efforts to deal with Separatists, Puritans, and Roman Catholics, and even more with the relocation of those problems on this side of the Atlantic, that the possibility of religious pluralism arose. Ever since, in England, and especially in America, we have had a population that was by and large Christian but which was divided among many Christian denominations. Between these denominations there has been a rivalry for the allegiance of people. There have been converts from one denomination to another. This kind of evangelism, as we said before, is proselytism. It has come to have a bad name, but it has at least this kind of legitimacy: at its best it is any effort to share with another the deepest insights one has been able to achieve.

The third period of history that we must examine began in this country in the eighteenth century. It is the history of the revival movement, whose key points include the two Great Awakenings. The movement has lasted down to the present, and it has been rightly said to have "dominated religion in the United States more than any other single influence" (*Westminster Dictionary of Church History*, p. 715). The Churches that were a part of the revival movement came to be designated as "evangelical," and, while they disagreed among themselves on many points, they did share one vastly important expectation, as Bernard A. Weisberger has pointed out in *They Gathered at the River* (Boston and Toronto: Little Brown & Co., 1958). He says:

They believed that those destined for eternal life went through a definite, palpable religious experience. First a man (or woman) felt a gnawing sense of guilt and wickedness, and then a frightening awareness that hell was an entirely just punishment for such a wretch as he. Thus "broken down before the Lord," the sinner, stripped of pride and self-esteem, was ready to throw himself on God's mercy. Now, if God had chosen him for salvation, he might read the promises in the Bible and feel that they applied to him. He could pass from being "convicted" of sin and "anxious" for his soul, to a state described as "hopeful." Lastly, he might have a climactic emotional experience, some special "baptism of the Spirit," some inward, unmistakable sign that pardon was extended and a crown of glory laid up for him in heaven. This was regeneration.

Revivalism has changed much over the two and a half centuries that it has lasted. In its earliest days, its advocates, such as Jonathan Edwards, insisted that a revival was a miracle sent from God and that there was nothing men could do to bring one on. By the time of the Beechers and the Finneys, however, revivals were thought of, not as something that God sent but rather as something that men arranged. Certain techniques could be practiced to insure that a revival occurred. It remained for Dwight L. Moody to apply to the revival the techniques of business: publicity, organization, and advertising. Billy Sunday added his characteristic touches, and Billy Graham has added electronic improvements in the way of PA systems, radio and TV programs, movies, and computers.

The main point I want to make about revivals is that by and large they have not been a means of converting non-Christians, but instead they have been a way of getting those who have grown up in a community that constructed reality in a Christian way to act on that construction more consistently. More than anything else, it has been the instrument for getting young people to assume adult responsibility in the congregation. It has also been a means of restoring inactive church members to active status. This means that revivalism is not so much a means of making new Christians as it is a way of renewing old ones. One can call that evangelism if he wishes, but it is very different from missionary work among non-Christians or even proselytism among those who belong to other Christian denominations.

The result of this brief historical survey has been to see that what usually is lumped together under the banner of evangelism are three distinct activities: (1) missionary work among non-Christians, whether they belong to other religions or have none; (2) proselytizing among those who are Christians of other denominations or points of view; and (3) the revival or renewal of those whose beliefs are the same as one's own but who do not have their lives organized around those beliefs.

I would like to make some general remarks about each of these three kinds of evangelism. First, missionary activity. We used to make a distinction between missions and evangelism, at least in popular usage if not in technical definition. Missions were foreign, at least to other cultures such as American Indians, but evangelism was among our own people. There are two reasons I do not like such a distinction. The first is that evangelism embraces proselytism and renewal as well as efforts to convert non-Christians, and it is easier to keep our meaning straight if we use evangelism only as the comprehensive term and speak of all efforts to win non-Christians, whether at home or abroad, as missionary activity.

Having said that, we are faced immediately with the necessity of saying something about the relative priorities of missionary activity here and overseas. We have undergone some humbling experiences in the last few years in relation to our foreign missions. I can remember my shock a few years ago when I made my first visit to the Overseas Department of our Episcopal Church Center in New York. I was shown into a huge room filled with desks, most of which were empty. Thus I saw, in a very graphic way, how drastically our overseas work had been cut back in the few short years since our national headquarters building had been erected. There are, of course, some good reasons for that. We had come to see how much that had passed for spreading the Gospel had been merely spreading western culture, and how closely missionary activity had been linked with the economic exploitation of the have-not peoples.

Reinhold Niebuhr used to warn us to be wary of any coincidence of altruism and self-interest. It was strange that we got around to noticing the shortcomings of our missionary program at the very time we were experiencing a budgetary crisis at home and could do very well with an excuse to cut down what we were spending to spread the faith abroad. Undoubtedly we need a different strategy of foreign missions than what we have had in the past. We have to recognize that there is an indigenous Church and clergy in most parts of the world today, and that some of what we used to call the "younger Churches" have a strength and zeal that puts Churches in the developed countries to shame. I think I am correct in remembering Archbishop Donald Arden of South Africa to have said that the Anglican Church in Africa is growing faster than anywhere else in the world and that there will soon be more black than white Anglicans in the world. We need to find ways to cooperate that will recognize our status as the junior if more affluent partner. As Bishop Stephen Neill said in his *History of Christian Missions* (New York: Penguin, 1964): "The age of missions is at an end; the age of mission has begun" (p. 572). Any concern for the conversion of non-Christians at home that is not accompanied by a willingness to give sacrificially for the same work in less affluent sections of the world will always lack credibility.

The other thing I have to say about missionary activity among non-Christians is that in many ways our situation at home is very similar to that in the Roman Empire. This is to say that the big rival to the Church for the allegiance of the hearts of men is not other religions, but no religion. In the ancient world, philosophy represented the only other total way of life to rival Christianity. Today the human rights movement probably comes closest to occupying that position. The basis of our appeal to people in that movement will have to be to show them that, all appearances to the contrary, the Christian Church offers them a far more effective channel for serving their fellow men than the secular movements to which they belong.

The main thing I would like to say about proselytism is to reemphasize a point that came up in our analysis of what takes place in evangelism: conversion is not the experience of an isolated individual but is always the transition of an individual from one group to another. For this reason, I think that for Episcopalians to model their evangelism on the techniques of the evangelicals is misleading in that it conveys unreal expectations about the Episcopal Church and that it fails to promise the real glories of our communion. We never experience Jesus in an unmediated form. Our experience of him is always understood in the categories of a particular Christian community.

I think I can illustrate this best by reference to a particular kind of experience many churchmen have had in recent years. They have been confronted by fellow Christians who have been caught up in one kind of renewal movement or another and who have asked them, "Do you have a personal relation with Jesus?" Now this kind of question is very upsetting to most Episcopalians because it is obvious to them that they do not have any such relation, if by that is meant a regular habit of prayer addressed to Jesus. And the nature of the question is that it suggests that they really ought to have such a relation, that they are less than a true Christian if they do not have it. Yet G. L. Prestige has shown in an excellent article that devotion to the sacred humanity of Christ did not develop in the Church until the twelfth century, with Bernard of Clairvaux and Francis of Assisi, and that it was opposed by Luther, Calvin, and the Anglican Reformers ("Eros: or, Devotion to the Sacred Humanity," *Fathers and Heretics* (Naperville, Ill: Allenson, 1940, pp. 180–207).

This means that the devotional tradition that sounds so normal and normative by the way the question is framed can be seen to be one of the byways of Christian devotion in its deviation from the usual assumption that prayer is addressed to the Father through the Son and in the Spirit. Prestige also goes on to warn about the dangers inherent in assuming that "some particular devotional practice not only is desirable in itself, but must be assumed to be grounded in a right theology because it 'encourages people to pray' or 'helps people in their prayers'" (p. 205). The point that I wish to make is that we use a vocabulary that represents a particular tradition of Christian living and we assume that it is objective, standard, and normative. This betrays the provincialism of our experience. Every technical term presupposes a community that uses language that way, and the vocabulary implies not only the content but also the community. It is impossible for us to borrow the vocabulary and techniques of evangelicals without taking over their whole system by implication. We should never do that unless we are very clear beforehand that such is in fact what we are doing and that it is what we want to do.

What I would like to say about the renewal of Episcopalians, at any rate, is that I believe that all of us, whether born into the Church or converts, have many basic convictions and experiences in common that were our reasons for becoming Episcopalians in the first place, or for ever getting enthusiastic about having been born that way. Our need for renewal grows out of the fact that we have gotten out of touch with those reasons. There are many causes for our having done so: sloth, original sin, preoccupation with other things. The most frequent cause, though, in my opinion, is that the last ten or fifteen years of living in our society has left us with an uneasy and uninvestigated sense that these central convictions have somehow been eroded by history, that they have suffered what someone has called "death by a thousand qualifications." I think, though, that many of us are now beginning to realize again that these really are our central convictions, these are the ideas around which our lives are organized. The best way that we can help others in the Church to be renewed is to help them to get back in touch with these convictions and to see if they do not continue to share them. I am sure that many of them would be relieved to discover that this is where they really are, that these are the assumptions that make them tick.

In order to check that out, I have tried to make a list of what these convictions are for me. I have entitled it, "Things I Cannot Deny."

1. Without God the world makes no sense.

2. Mankind and individual men are estranged from God and do not fulfill his purpose for them.

3. In Jesus, God not only showed us what reconciled life is like, but also made it a possibility for us.

4. The possibility of reconciliation is not extended to each of us as isolated individuals, but is available through the reconciled community, the Church.

5. Our life in that community and our participation in that reconciliation is begun in baptism and sustained in the Eucharist.

6. Our life in that community today is in continuity with its life not only in the apostolic period but also in all intervening periods.

7. Reconciled living is expressed in the worship of God, fellowship with brother Christians, and love for those outside the Church; which, in turn, is expressed in (a) trying to share with them our life in Christ, and (b) expressing in action our concern for their physical, psychological, and social well-being.

8. Worship of God requires the most beautiful expression of which we are capable.

9. While all true religion touches people at their emotional depths, intensity of emotion is not the criterion by which we evaluate the truth of beliefs. Rather, theological content is required to give clarity and structure to religious experience.

10. Moral behavior is not a matter of a "new law," whether trivial

Evangelism in the Church: An Overview

or noble, but is life lived in self-giving love: love for the Father with our whole being, and love for the neighbor equal to what we have for ourselves. The neighbor is recognized to include both society as a whole and any individual who needs our help.

11. Since all truth comes from God, truths that are being discovered today are not inconsistent with and can be no threat to "the faith once delivered to the saints."

A quick look at this list shows us that various items on it are more appropriate to one form of evangelism than another: to missionary work, proselytism, or renewal. The first three statements, which have to do with the existence of God, the pervasiveness of sin, and our need for divine assistance in overcoming it, is the good news we have to bring to non-Christians. Evangelicals who see conversion as a private transaction between God and an individual man or woman need to know that it is the Church that is the sphere of the divine-human encounter. In number five we remind those caught up in the subjectivity of religious experience of the objectivity of the sacraments. Those who know the Church only in a culturally conditioned modern expression are reminded in the sixth statement that the past life of the Church is a criterion by which the completeness of its contemporary manifestations must be judged. In number seven we are reminded that Christian behavior involves obligations to God, fellow Christians, and the world at large. Number eight bears witness to our Anglican experience of the holiness of beauty. In the ninth statement we try to do justice to the importance of emotion in religion without giving any ground to emotionalism. The tenth conviction sternly resists any tendency to revert to an Old Testament standard of law rather than grace, a tendency to which all denominations are far too prone. Number eleven firmly opposes any ghetto mentality on the part of Christians and declares us to be open to secular as well as religious truth.

I may have left the impression that Christians who come out of denominations that have been evangelical in the narrow sense in their past are still in that situation, that only Episcopalians share all of these eleven basic convictions, and that Episcopalians have nothing to learn from their Christian brothers of other traditions. Obviously, none of that is so. Reality, as it has been constructed by each community, has been in a constant process of legitimation necessitated by our life together in one society, and all of us have had to come to terms with the truth and experiences to which other traditions bear witness. Many Methodists, for instance, would feel that they have far more in common with my eleven basic convictions than with the description of the faith of my home town when I was a boy. By the same token, Episcopalians, and even Roman Catholics by the thousands, have learned from their evangelical brothers and sisters about the vitality that can come through the charismatic and evangelical movements of renewal. For all of this, we must all give thanks to God.

On the subject of method I have nothing original to say. Evangelistic methods that seem to me consistent with our basic convictions are ones that were common in the fifties when I was a young parish priest. The very best one is to invite someone to church. I am convinced that there are thousands of spiritually hungry souls who will experience what Edmund Wilson in another context called "the shock of recognition." In *Merrily on High* (New York: Morehouse, 1973) Fr. Colin Stephenson, the late warden of the Shrine of Our Lady of Walsingham, tells how life came to disabuse him of his romantic fantasy that all it would take to convert the world to Anglo-Catholicism was to give everyone a chance to behold the baroque splendor of its services. It obviously would not convert everyone if all were to attend Episcopal services, but I am sure that there must be many people like me on whom that experience had such a powerful impact. It still seems to me to be what we are about and that the surest way for people to discover if they should make their home with us is to come and see.

Beyond that, I think the right kind of tracts are invaluable. The Diocese of Northwest Texas has prepared one called "Those Crazy Episcopalians" that I like very much. And I would love to see someone reissue the magnificently simple, graphic, and sound strip-cartoon tracts that Bede House in Canada put out in the fifties. Then, too, it seems to me to be about time to revive the preaching mission.

But I really do not wish to get too preoccupied with techniques and methods. The main thing we really need to do, I think, is to put Episcopalians back in touch with their own most cherished convictions. When that is done, anything can happen. What Harnack said about the expansion of the early Church is still true today: "A living faith requires no special 'methods' for its propagation; on it sweeps over every obstacle."

chapter 9

THE FUTURE FOR EVANGELISM

Louis J. Willie

Go forth . . . and teach! It is the duty of a Christian to be an evangelist. This obligation is placed upon us by Christ himself when he tells his followers to "Go forth therefore and make all nations my disciples; baptize men everywhere in the name of the Father and the Son and the Holy Spirit, and teach them to observe all that I have commanded you" (Matt. 28:19-20). Again from the Book of Common Prayer we are told that our "bounden duty is to follow Christ . . . and to work and pray and give for the spread of His Kingdom." A close look at evangelism from a biblical perspective makes us aware that the obligation to spread the Gospel has been imposed upon the Christian by Christ himself, and the Christian has a duty to discharge it.

What is evangelism? This question should be answered in order for the reader to understand what the writer means when he uses the word. Evangelism comes from a Greek word meaning to announce good news. The dictionary defines evangelism as a preaching of, or zealous effort to, spread the Gospel. The Committee on Evangelism of the General Convention of the Episcopal Church in 1973 defined evangelism as "the presentation of Jesus Christ, in the power of the Holy Spirit, in such ways that persons may be led to believe in Him as Savior and follow Him as Lord within the fellowship of the Church."

What is an evangelist? The Bible says "This gospel of the Kingdom will be proclaimed throughout the earth as a testimony to all nations" (Matt. 24:14). The evangelist is a witness for Jesus Christ who is willing to proclaim the Gospel of Christ to the world. The evangelist may be an ordained minister or a lay person. Whether he is ordained or not is not nearly as important as his knowledge of the Gospel of Jesus, his enthusiasm for proclaiming that Gospel, and his willingness to be let God use him as a witness to testify to the power and truth of the Gospel. The evangelist, therefore, is any member of the Christian Church who (1) believes the good news he has heard about our Lord Jesus Christ; (2) believes that he is obligated to bear witness to this good news both locally and worldwide; (3) has personally experienced the power of God's Holy Spirit in his life and in the lives of others; and (4) is willing to spread the good news of our Lord with confidence and with zeal.

What is the state of evangelism in the Church today? While much of what is written here concerns what is going on in the Episcopal Church, I am aware that the evangelistic efforts of my branch of the faith are duplicated and perhaps exceeded by other Christian bodies. I see more and more people from all walks of life turning to the Church to give some direction and stability to their lives. I also see a willingness on the part of Christians to share the joy and the peace which Christ has brought into their lives. Prayer groups and Bible study groups are being formed in increasing numbers across the United States. Men and women are meeting every day in the week in small groups—at work, in private homes, and in churches—praying, studying Christian literature, reading their Bibles, sharing with one another what Jesus Christ is doing in their lives, and thanking and praising God for the wonderful things he is doing in the world.

There is other evidence that the desire to know Christ and to make him known is alive throughout the land. The Billy Graham Crusades continue to fill large stadiums in major metropolitan areas all over these United States. People come to hear the Gospel proclaimed in simple language and with enthusiasm and conviction. Mr. Graham's televised crusades attract millions of listeners who, if they choose to, could turn off their television sets or dial another channel. Other television evangelists have very high audience ratings. Gospel and religious programs on radio attract a broad variety of listeners. There are some radio stations and cable television channels which are all religious in their programming. If these stations did not have a receptive and loyal audience listening to their output, they could not exist. In the Episcopal Church we find enthusiastic support for evangelistic preaching missions such as those conducted by Canon Brian Green, the Rev. Robert Hall, the Rev. Rufus Womble, the Rev. Charles Murphy, and others. The Anglican Fellowship of Prayer continues to grow and to have a positive effect on the lives of many through its programs of prayer, teaching, and fellowship. Pews Action, a coalition of evangelistic groups within the Episcopal Church, was very effective in its Christian witness at the General Convention of the Episcopal Church in 1973. I am sure that the zeal and commitment of this same group to spread the Gospel will have an even greater impact on the General Convention of 1976.

The Future for Evangelism 79

What is the future of evangelism? The evidence accumulates that interest in evangelism in this country and the world is rising. I am therefore optimistic about its future for several reasons. The first one is based on a promise of Jesus Christ. In the Gospel According to Matthew, Jesus says to his followers after commanding them to teach the whole world about him: "I am with you always, to the end of time" (Matt. 28:20). With this assurance, the forces of evil cannot stop or hinder the work of the Church for any extended period of time. Admittedly, in some countries behind the Iron Curtain, the work of witnesses for Christ has been effectively curtailed. There are reports, however, from within other countries which have been most hostile to the Church that the Gospel of Jesus Christ is being spread. The evangelist is at work, although in a clandestine manner, and his work is being done at great risk to his freedom and possibly to his life. There are many examples of men and women on this earth whose lives have been changed in a positive way by the Gospel; and to let it die because of political oppression is unthinkable. There are saints in the Church today who are willing to suffer to keep alive the spirit of Christ throughout the earth.

A second reason for my optimism lies in the battered condition of society and the world in the mid 1970s. During the past twenty years technological and social changes have become unmanageable for large numbers of people. Wars, threats of war, terrorism, starvation, inflation coupled with recession, and higher than normal unemployment, and many other examples of business, political, and spiritual instability have literally driven many people to question the values upon which their security has been built. This questioning of old institutions, old values, old priorities, becomes fertile ground for the work of the evangelist. His values, being rooted in Jesus Christ, have not failed him. Through all the changes of this world the Christian witness is at peace. He has joy in his heart. He is not exempt from pain and suffering. The difference is that he has his Lord's grace to sustain and comfort him when the problem of pain and suffering does arise. The opportunities presented to the evangelist for teaching frightened and disillusioned people about the grace of God and what it means to them are unlimited. The evangelist can proclaim with the conviction of Henry Francis Lyte in his well-known hymn, "change and decay in all around I see, O Thou who changest not, abide with me (The 1940 Hymnal, #467).

The third reason for my optimism lies in the speed with which religious organizations have responded to the needs of suffering humanity in many parts of the globe. This is especially true when great human need is brought to the attention of the public through the mass media. Religious bodies, and other organizations motivated by religious principles, have led the way in alleviating hunger and the devastation brought on by great natural disasters such as droughts, floods, earthquakes, and fires. God wants us to feed the body as well as the mind. The early and continuing response which the Church makes to those in need says to the stricken that somebody cares. When we share what we have with another of less good fortune, we are witnessing to the command of Christ to feed the hungry, clothe the naked, help the sick, show hospitality to strangers, and show sympathy with prisoners, the outcasts, and the downtrodden.

The Next Decade—Which Direction? In this essay on evangelism, I would like to share with my brothers and sisters in the Episcopal Church my feeling about some directions the Church should take and some goals I would like to see it adopt and accomplish. These goals are not new, nor are they revolutionary. They are a statement of what Christians have believed for centuries. It is my hope that as we move to tell the good news of Jesus Christ to the people of this country and to the world beyond its shores, we will tell the truth with the courage and authority of one who knows where he is going and what he is talking about. I want to see the Episcopal Church at the national, diocesan, and parish levels adopt and pursue some simple, uncomplicated, but modest action programs. If these action programs are vigorously executed, the voice of God's witnesses will be amplified with greater effectiveness and influence. There are several plans I would like to see enacted and supported with enthusiasm.

Action Program No. 1—Triple Church membership and Church attendance by 1986.

For many years I have heard Church people talk about "winning souls for Christ." This implies bold and vigorous action. We follow our "winning" proclamation with what I consider a contradiction: "Let's not worry about numbers." I say let us be very much concerned with numbers! The numbers of souls brought into the Church are a good indication of how well or how poorly we are doing. Can you imagine an athletic team entering a contest against a tough opponent with the coach stating that he wants his team to win but that he is not concerned with the score? The more people we bring into the Church and the more nominal or lapsed members we encourage to attend church regularly, the stronger the Church will be as a force against evil. A man, woman, boy, or girl inside the fold of Christ's Church has a better chance for eternal salvation than does one who is outside. Since zeal for the extension of the Church is one of the characteristics that distinguishes the Christians from the rest of society, this program should receive a high priority.

Action Program No. 2—Church financial support will be a percentage of the communicant's "take home pay" from all sources.

If the Church is going to discharge its obligation to evangelize those

The Future for Evangelism

who are near and those who are in faraway places, it must have adequate funds. It has been said that the reason some people have joined the Episcopal Church is because there is little talk about money. I say let's talk about money and its place in the Church. Unless the Church is supported out of the personal incomes of its members, it will close its doors. The Church does not get a free ride. It has to pay its expenses and debts with legal tender. It has to pay its professionals who are giving their full time to God's work. It must respond when human suffering cries out for relief. When drought has left starvation in its wake, when earthquakes, winds, floods, and disasters have ravaged whole regions, the Church must send material relief in addition to its prayers. Material relief and the cost of its transportation to the stricken must be paid for with dollars. Let us, therefore, cease to feel guilty and timid about the role of money in the advancement of God's kingdom. I believe that if one is financially responsible about the support of the Church, he will be financially responsible in the other areas of life. I want to see the Church boldly teach its members that their treasure belongs where their heart is. If one's heart is in Christ Jesus and his Church, a percentage of his money should be there also.

Action Program No. 3—Support for the Church and other organizations of community relief with regular and budgeted gifts of the communicant's time and skills.

No Christian witness will satisfy his need to make Christ known to all men by the simple act of writing a check. He must be personally involved with the work of God's Church and with the alleviation of human suffering. If God's work is to be done on earth, it must be done by the acts of women and men, girls and boys. Nothing is expressed here to imply that every witness must go to foreign or domestic mission fields, or that everyone should be personally involved in hospital, prison, or volunteer work requiring special skills. In these areas, of course, the evangelist will make a gift of money to finance a surrogate or representative. I am assuming that, barring the disabilities of bad health, every member of the Church, from teen-agers up, has some time and skill which the Church or other organizations for community relief can use on a regular basis. There are thousands of organizations, both Church-related and secular, including schools, which are responding to human needs. They need volunteers to do the work they have been called to do. It is the duty of the Church to remind its members of their obligation to serve God and man. No one spoke more eloquently on the subject of service than did Jesus when speaking to his disciple. He said, "Whosoever would be first among you shall be your servant, even as the Son of man came not to be ministered unto but to minister" (Matt. 20:27,28). Our Lord demonstrated what personal service means when he washed the feet of his disciples and said to them, "I have set you an example: you are to do as I have done" (John 13:12–17).

Action Program No. 4—Confessing Christ and witnessing to the Catholic Faith.

What wonderful and precious gifts have been given to us by the Church. The sacraments, the Bible, prophets, saints, the creeds, and traditions have all been handed down to us by past generations. Some of the great Christian principles would never have reached us if other Christians in years gone by had not been willing to die to defend the faith and proclaim the Gospel.

Our national, diocesan, and parish leaders must speak out without fear in their condemnation of sin and wrongdoing as it exists all around us. The matter of witnessing to the faith in the face of sin is not a matter for leaders alone. It is the duty of all Christians to witness against sin wherever it appears. George D. Carleton says in his book that "bearing witness to the Catholic faith is not merely by spoken words, but also and chiefly by living true to Christian and Catholic principles in our daily life in the world."[1] The Church must constantly remind its members of their obligation to stand for truth every day in whatever state they might find themselves. Christian evangelists cannot live in isolation. They must be a part of society—working, playing, living, and dying just like everybody else. The witness lives, even as Christ did, among the people he serves. The Church has experimented with all sorts of things since its beginning—some have succeeded, others have failed. I am calling for a nationally supported program in which the Church calls its members to be strong moral forces—by word and deed—in this country and beyond. There can be little debate about this being the Church's forte.

There is a confidence gap between people and the institutions that serve them. A Harris poll taken the first quarter of 1976 shows that religion has the confidence of the population in the 20 percent range.[2] Religion has plenty of company in this loss of confidence matter, for business, medicine, government, the press, and others have suffered also. If we dedicate ourselves to being the Church and following the teachings of our Lord, I believe that millions will begin to reassess their position about the validity of the Church. I am fearful that too many men and women see the conduct of Christians as being no different from non-Christians. They also see the institutional Church as being no different from its secular counterparts. Committed Christian witnesses can make the Church the light to guide lost souls to Christ. The time to act is now. Let us pray the prayer of Harry Emerson Fosdick: "Grant us wisdom, grant courage, that we fail not man nor Thee."

NOTES

1. George D. Carleton, *The Kings Highway* (London: Church Literature Association, 1963), pp.204,205.
2. *Research Institute Recommendations*, March 26, 1976, p.3.

chapter 10

CHURCH EDUCATION FOR TOMORROW

John H. Westerhoff III

It is a truism that Christian faith and education are inevitable companions. Wherever living faith exists, there is a community endeavoring to sustain and transmit that faith. Still, an accurate description of education in the Church today is almost impossible. Generalizations are meaningless. Evangelical Protestant, Orthodox, Roman Catholic, and mainline Protestant Churches appear to confront unique situations, though perhaps the greatest crisis is being experienced among the mainline bodies (my own tradition).

THE NEED FOR RADICAL CHANGES

Nevertheless, I would argue that while situations differ, the understandings, purposes, and theological foundations upon which all Christian groups engage in education are shaking. While a host of builders attempt, with varying degrees of success, to shore them up, there is a dearth of architects engaged in designing new structures.

This conviction is not entirely new. *Colloquy,* a magazine on education in the Church in society, was born in 1968. For eight years, as its founder-editor, I advocated the need for radical changes in Church education. In 1970, just before the walls of mainline Protestant Church education began to show their cracks, I wrote a short tract, *Values for Tomorrow's Children* (Pilgrim, 1970), which boldly suggested that a radical alternative for Church education was needed for the future. In *A Colloquy on Christian Education* (Pilgrim, 1972) and *Generation to Generation* (Pilgrim, 1974), I expanded that thesis. I have now concluded that it is not enough simply to conceive of alternatives for Church education; fundamental issues once clearly resolved need to be explored afresh. No longer can we assume that the educational understandings that have informed us, the purposes that have inspired our efforts, or the theological foundations that have undergirded our programs are adequate for today.

During the early decades of the twentieth century, the religious education movement was a major force in American Christianity, but the future is uncertain. While many realize that we can't go home again, few can agree on the direction we need to take. I suggest, as a way of beginning, that evangelicals and liberals, "high" and "low" Church persons, Roman Catholics and Protestants, Christians and those of other faiths stop warring, ignoring each other, or passing each other in the night, and begin to share perspectives and convictions. Coalitions of local Church lay persons, Church education professionals, clergy, Church bureaucrats, and academics need to begin working together more closely.

As one contribution to this end, divinity schools will need to reconstitute the theoretical study of religion and education. New centers for Church education need to emerge where scholars in numerous fields can engage in research and development around foundational issues. Here and there this is already taking place: Our work at Duke University and that of my friends James Fowler at Harvard, David Stewart at Pacific School of Religion, and Berard Marthaler at the Catholic University of America, among others. The challenge, however, is before all of us. These reflections are offered to stimulate our common task. The stakes are high, for education is central to the Christian community's life and mission.

THE PUBLIC SCHOOL AS MODEL

In every age, in every endeavor, some agreed-upon frame of reference has informed the Church's education efforts. Since the turn of the century, Church education has operated according to a "schooling-instruction" paradigm. While admitting that learning takes place in many ways, Church education has functionally equated the context of education with schooling and the means of education with formal instruction. The public school has been the model, and insights from secular pedagogy and psychology provided guides. For Protestants, a school with teachers, subject matter, curriculum resources, age-graded classes, supplies, equipment, classrooms, and, if possible, a professional educator has been the norm. For Roman Catholics, parochial schools or some other form of catechetics are traditional. Within this understanding, creative responses have been made to the Church's educational ministry.

There are, however, numerous anomalies in that paradigm: Characteristically, only large, well-to-do churches with professional leadership have been able to meet adequately the full requirements of the Church School, and even they have begun to question their results. Schools and formal instruction seem effective for teaching about Christianity but not for enabling growth in faith. The crucial ecology of institutions—community, public (or parochial) school, home, and church—which once unconsciously supported the Church School CED program cannot accomplish what it once took five interrelated institutions to do. And most serious, the processes of religious socialization have been systematically kept outside the purview of Church Educators. The result has been catastrophic, for we all know that faith and values are not primarily the result of formal instruction. Indeed, the hidden curriculum in our lives is often more influential than the formal curriculum of schools.

We have too easily linked the ways of secular education with religion. Dependence upon the practice, rhetoric, and norms of secular education is risky business, for, there is something unique about education in religious communities. Yet when we have faced new problems, our typical response has been to focus Church education even more sharply on formal teaching and learning, naïvely believing that it is possible with new knowledge and techniques to build a workable school for the Church, train an adequate number of capable teachers, and provide more useful curriculum resources for quality Church education. In bondage to this inadequate understanding, we interpret any small success or reversal of existing negative trends in Church schooling as a confirmation of the old paradigm's validity.

THE NATURAL CONTEXT OF EDUCATION

In my opinion it is the paradigm itself which is bankrupt, not the attempts at educational reform which issue from it. An alternative paradigm, not merely an alternative program, is needed. I am currently developing a "community of faith-enculturation" paradigm in which the total life of a radical faith community becomes the context of education, and being Christian together becomes the means to achieve it. We need to center our educational concern on the Church's rites and rituals, the formal and informal experiences persons have within the community, and the actions engaged in and encouraged by the community in the world.

While a new paradigm needs to maintain a necessary particularity for education—deliberate, systematic, and sustained efforts—and a place for schooling and instruction, it must broaden Church education to include, consciously and intentionally, as the primary context and means of education, every aspect of our individual and corporate lives within an intentional, covenanting, tradition-bearing faith community. Only as we rethink the radical nature of Christian community and reform our institutions so that they might faithfully strive to transmit their cumulative tradition through ritual and life, to nurture and convert persons to Christian faith through common experience and interaction, and to prepare and motivate persons for individual and corporate action in society can true Christian education emerge.

To accomplish this end, we need to ask what it means to "be Christian together," and how it is that persons develop mature faith. Our question cannot be "How can someone teach someone else about the Christian faith?" but "How can we be Christian, individually and corporately, with others in the world?" To answer that question we need to address faith's relationship to religion, our corporate selves, and society. Thus a new paradigm not only makes possible new forms and means for Church education but also suggests new questions and answers as to our purposes.

NURTURE OR CONVERSION?

Historically, Church education has vacillated between a concern for conversion and a concern for nurture. With the birth of the schooling-instructional paradigm, nurture became the dominant underlying purpose in the rhetoric of Roman Catholic and mainline Protestant Church education. Characteristically, Christian faith was understood in terms of nurture, which functionally corresponded to a gradual process of schooling. Church educators proceeded to develop a program of education that moved from baptism through instruction to confirmation—or, more accurately, to institutional initiation. At the same time evangelical Protestant Churches, also enamored of the schooling-instructional paradigm, described personal conversion as their purpose, not designed educational programs that used instruction to move persons to an early baptism and commitment. Neither side could affirm the other's purpose, though both depended upon the same paradigm. Both, I contend, have made a serious error.

Support for nurture as the sole purpose of Church education is found in a single phrase in Horace Bushnell's *Christian Nurture:* "A child is to grow up a Christian and never know himself or herself as being otherwise." It is interesting that little attention is given to the fact that, as the last of the Puritans, Bushnell referred in his dictum only to the children of the saints. I contend that the Church can no longer surrender to the illusion that child nurture, in and of itself, can or will rekindle the fire of Christian faith either in persons or in the Church.

We have expected too much of nurture. At its very best, nurture makes possible institutional incorporation. We can nurture persons into institutional religion, but not into mature Christian faith. The Christian faith by its very nature demands conversion. We do not gradually educate persons to be Christian. Of course, conversion can be, and indeed often has been, misunderstood and overemphasized to the neglect of nurture, but that does not justify our disregarding it as the one necessary purpose of Christian education.

In one sense we all inherit faith. We are nurtured or socialized into certain ways of understanding the world and our lives, and into particular goals for life and guides for conduct. One style of faith typical of children but also necessary for life is founded upon a deep sense of belonging to a community in which faith is expressed through the "heart" and belief is dependent upon external authority. Persons need to be nurtured into a community's faith and life, its memory and goals, its story and way. There is a basic need for religious experience and the developing of the affections. But persons, if they are to grow in faith, also need to be aided and encouraged to judge, to question, and even to doubt that faith. They need to be given the opportunity to experiment with and reflect upon alternative understandings and to learn what it means to commit their lives to causes and persons. We must never depreciate the important intellectual aspect of Christian faith. Only after a long adolescent struggle with doubt and an honest consideration of alternatives can a person truly say, "I believe." And only then is a person enabled to live the radical political, economic, and social life of the Christian in the world.

FROM FAITH GIVEN TO FAITH OWNED

Conversion is therefore best understood as a radical turning from faith given (through nurture) to faith owned. Conversion is radical because it implies ownership and the corresponding transformation of our lives. It implies a turning from one style of faith to another and, as such, is characterized by a total reorientation in our thinking, feeling, and willing. That is why, historically, conversion is not singularly an emotional outburst, nor a once-and-for-all occasion to be dated and described. Rather it is more like a long series of significant changes in our total behavior and enlightenments—changes that can be identified only in retrospect. Neither is conversion an isolated event devoid of an element of nurture. Nurture and conversion are a unified whole. Parenthetically, neither the liberal who has nurtured persons into Church membership nor the evangelical who has nurtured persons into accepting the Church's religion has taken faith and the relationship between nurture and conversion seriously.

Neither the pietist who has no commitment to the struggle for justice and righteousness in the world of institutional life nor the social activist who has no personal commitment to Christ is converted to mature Christian faith. True conversion—authentic Christian life—is personal and social life lived on behalf of God's reign in the political, social, and economic world. One cannot be nurtured into such life—not in this world. Every culture strives to socialize persons to live in harmony with life as it is. The culture calls upon its religious institutions to bless the status quo, and upon religion's educational institutions to nurture persons into acceptance of it.

But God calls his people to be signs of Shalom, the vanguard of God's kingdom, a community of cultural change. To reach the conviction that such countercultural life is our Christian vocation, and to be enabled to live such a corporate existence in but not of the world, necessitates conversion as well as nurture.

Once again we need to understand that both conversion and nurture have a place in Church education if such education is to be Christian. Our sole concern for nurture has contributed to our losing both an evangelical power and a social dynamic. While rejecting a sterile revivalism, we constructed a false evangelism through nurture. Church education for conversion means helping persons to see that they are called, not only to believe the Church's affirmation that Jesus is the Christ but to commit their lives to him and to live as apostles and disciples in the world. And considering that task brings us face to face with some basic theological issures.

A THEOLOGY FOR TODAY

Once again, those responsible for Church education are confronted with a crucial decision: What theological orientation will inform their labors? Church education is a dependent discipline—dependent upon theological underpinnings which both judge and inspire its work. On occasion we have forgotten that fact and, at our peril, relied upon insights from philosophy, the social sciences, or general education. What theological system will inspire Church education during the next decade is a central issue to be resolved.

The religious education movement, a mainline Protestant Church endeavor, was the offspring of liberal theology and the Second Gospel. George Albert Coe's Social Theory of Religious Education (New York: Arno Press, 1969) best translated the liberal understanding to the area of Church education. When neo-orthodoxy emerged, it consumed the education enterprise. My predecessor at Duke, H. Shelton Smith, asserted the important unity of education and theology and sought to build a bridge between liberalism's concern with the social order and neo-orthodoxy's concern for the tradition. But there was no acceptable theology to hold these two together; hence they have remained essentially estranged up to the present.

Today proponents of a variety of theological positions are vying for attention. Conservative, liberal, new reformation, liberation, hermeneutical, process, and eschatological theologies all speak to part of the tradition. From my perspective, "liberation theology" (especially as seen in the work of my colleague Frederick Herzog) is the most promising because it makes possible a synthesis. It provides a base for new coalitions between Roman Catholics and Protestants (witness the ecumenical character of its adherents), liberals and conservatives (witness the continuing concerns of the World Council of Churches and the evangelicals' Chicago Declaration), majorities and minorities (witness the numerous theological works written from black, feminist, Latin American, and Anglo perspectives), and therefore can become an acceptable, sound theological foundation for Church education.

In any case, a workable theology to undergird Church education today should have certain characteristics. It should both affirm a concern for experience and the religious affections, and be founded upon a historicist perspective. Further, it should unite the Christian tradition with a radical concern for social justice.

To restrict religion to the immediate relations between an individual and God or to an individual's relationship with another individual—that is, to a religion of personal salvation—is heresy. To neglect the world and institutional life is to deny the sovereignty of God over the whole of life, and to practice an idolatry which confines God to our individual existence and limits the Christian life to individual behavior is to leave the world to the principalities and powers.

A common motif for a relevant theology needs to be centered upon action and reflection arising out of a commitment to Jesus Christ as Lord and the desire both to understand and to act with God in the light of a corrupt and changing world. Needed is a foundation for uniting a radical understanding of God's action in history with radical individual and corporate discipleship in the world—namely, praxis (reflective action) which results from depth experience, the spiritual life, and the interiorization of faith through meditation, prayer, and corporate worship.

HOLISTIC EDUCATION

An adequate theology for Church education today will not only raise questions about schooling and instruction but will push us to ask what we uniquely have to bring to and receive from each other as followers of the crucified God. It will affirm the centrality of the will, which unites thought and passion in action. It will further elevate conversion to a position of new importance and affirm the possibility of our being grasped and radically turned around so that we might commit our lives to new goals for individual and social life.

A theology for our day must call our lives into question by reminding us that God's message of mercy is also a message of judgment. It must question our understanding of mission and ask that we not only help our neighbor but also equip ourselves to change the social, economic, and political structures that make help necessary. Such a theology will ask that we be more concerned for the transformation of persons and society than for the growth of Church membership or the numbers of those who say they believe in Jesus. Thus it will place faith commitment above both institutional religion and pietism. As such, it will require of us new understandings of religious community and new holistic forms of Christian education.

A myopic concern for nurture, understood as schooling and instruction undergirded by increasingly vague pluralistic theologies, will not be adequate for framing the future of Church education. A new paradigm encompassing the radical nature of Christian community, with conversion and nurture as its purpose and with an experiential, historicist, liberation theology undergirding it, can provide us with a framework for our educational mission and ministry in the next decade.

I offer these first thoughts in the hope that others will join the dialogue. The issues and their solution belong to all of us, and the stakes are high. A first word has been spoken, and the last should not be hurried.

chapter 11

FULFILLING THE BODY OF CHRIST

Philip Deemer

During the past three years in my work in planning, producing, and editing *New Life,* a magazine concerned largely with renewal in the Episcopal Church, I have found myself continually excited and frightened about the future of the Church. That which is frightening has caused me some despair, while that which is exciting has given me much hope. Since as Christians we are a people of hope—Jesus Christ being our very hope and salvation—I find myself optimistic about the future of the Church. However, that is not to say that there do not still exist doubts that those elements which I find frightening may win out after all, but I pray not.

What causes me despair is the existence of some very severe extremes on both sides of many issues. On one hand, one can find pockets of concern, renewal, and growth which exist in the Church, but which in all too many cases exist around the personality cult of a particular Church leader rather than around the person of *the* leader, Jesus Christ. On the other hand, one finds many pockets where the concept of renewal is perceived as automatically changing everything, throwing out all of the old accustomed ways and cherished usages and substituting something completely foreign to the backgrounds of many Church people. These pockets of resistance are usually so closed that there is little chance for growth of any kind.

More than any other factor, it would appear that these extremes on both ends are caused by our system of education—or lack of it, I should say—within our Church. Those who are following personality cults are frequently doing so because the personality involved is not teaching them

Fulfilling the Body of Christ

that they should be following Jesus Christ instead of their human leader. Those who are resisting any kind of change are frequently doing so because no one is teaching them what the proposed changes are about and the resisters, very understandably, come to feel that change is being forced upon them. I remember reading in the parish bulletin of a small church in New England the rector's announcement that the parish was going to use the "Green Book" for the next four Sundays because the bishop had asked them to do so. Needless to say, there was virtually no enthusiasm for the idea and consequently there was no real teaching, pro or con, about what the Green Book represented or offered; the result was, quite naturally, an expression of "Thank God that's over. We did our duty and made the bishop happy." Nowhere in the process was there any form of educating the parishioners to what it was all about.

We miss the boat this way time and again and these opportunities apply whether one is talking about the Church's life on a purely spiritual level, instruction in Sunday schools, parish life, liturgical changes, involvement in social activism, training in our seminaries, understanding and developing stewardship, missionary policies—or what have you. The categories can go on and on. Most concerned people in the Church know them as well as I do, and probably better.

Much of the present situation in religious and/or spiritual education is a reality that comes from the Church trying to preserve itself. In a process of years, and I truly feel that this process goes back for quite a number of years, we have been developing a system whereby the institutional Church has preserved its institutional self as its main priority. At the same time it has offered only a token effort toward preserving and building itself as the body of Christ.

Some years ago I attended a parish on the periphery of a ghetto in the Bronx. It was the first and only time I have ever been there, but I have always remembered the inspiration of the rector's sermon that morning. Just several weeks prior there had been a series of fires in the Bronx, including several churches. It was suspected that at least some had been the result of arson. These circumstances prompted the priest that morning to say that he hoped no fire would ever destroy their church building, but he vowed that if that ever happened the congregation would meet the following Sunday in a nearby park (it was, fortunately, summer when he said this) and the parish's life would go on. He told his congregation that they would go on because they were part of the Church, they were part of the body of Christ, and that while buildings were fine and desirable, they had absolutely nothing to do with being a full member of the body of Christ.

One could see from the responses on the faces of the people in that congregation that they knew and understood what their priest was teaching them. Here was a case where the people were being educated to know themselves and to know the Church more as the body of Christ than as just an institution.

In the past three years, through the pages of *New Life,* I have written some strong editorials. Strong editorials almost always bring strong reactions, both favorable and unfavorable, and I have received my share of both and have welcomed them. Some people have come to think of me as wanting to destroy the institution of the Church. Nothing could be further from the truth!

Rather, I believe—almost more than I believe anything else about the future of the Church—that as the Church sees itself more and more as the body of Christ, it will grow, strengthen, prosper, *and* lead its people; and it won't have to worry about preserving the institution. A band of Christians in this Episcopal Church which grows ever larger in its spiritual depth and its commitment to the Lord Jesus Christ, who is indeed its chief pastor, is not really going to have to worry about where the money will come from, what liturgy is being used, or which person is celebrating it. A band of Christians who are trying ever harder to live out the Gospel as our Lord lived it isn't going to have to worry about leadership or budgets or social activism. Those things will all grow quite naturally out of the commitment of the people of God coming to accept themselves within the Church which sees itself *as the body of Christ.*

Where does this leave us right now? Well, unfortunately it leaves many persons in the Church in a sense of apathy. In so many cases the institutional Church has been so concerned with preserving the structure that it has forgotten its ultimate reason for existence: to win people's hearts and souls to living their lives in the fullness of the Gospel of the Lord. The Church has so easily fallen into today's trap, so prevalent in many aspects of our society, of conforming itself to the world. If all the Church is going to be is just one segment *of* the world, then, understandably, many of its members may feel themselves justified in saying: "Who needs it?"

The answer is, of course, that *they* need it. We all do. And that is where the element of hope lies for the future. We *can*—indeed we *must*—become an ever-growing band of Christians, growing into the fullness of the body of Christ.

But how?

I don't have any pat answers for that. Some other people may have, but I don't. I have some hopes and a vision of the Church reaching the fullness of the body of Christ, but I don't have any certain answers about the way to achieve it. It would seem to me, however, that one of the prime considerations would be that of education—or reeducation, if you will. We must find a way to teach or reteach people that the Church is the body of Christ. We can have the most perfect structure in the world and we can

Fulfilling the Body of Christ

build or maintain some magnificent architectural wonders, but what good will it all be if there are no believing people? As things stand now, without increased stewardship we are not going to be able to maintain for much longer the structure we already have or those superlative buildings we have already constructed. And what is stewardship but understanding that all that we have comes from God and our need to live a responsible life with what God has given us?

If others in the Church are like I am, we are all creatures prone to staying within the comfortable boundaries of the knowledge which we have absorbed through the years. We may be open to acquiring new knowledge but we aren't too prone to change. We like being comfortable people. Sometimes, however, things that have become merely routine in our lives have become comfortable because we have learned them that way.

Take Lent, for instance. Many persons over thirty grew up being taught by the Church that we ought to give up something for Lent. There is nothing wrong in that teaching. Certainly Lent is a penitential season in which a more sacrificial way of life is not inappropriate. So, as children, we gave up candy or the movies, peanut butter or roller skating for Lent, and we believed that we were doing something good. And so we were. But how many of us were ever taught, as more and more of our children are being taught today, that Lent is also a time for taking on something additional, whether it be something of a spiritual nature or some voluntary act within our parish or community?

This is an example of where education is starting to lead us, because it is not only our children who are being taught today that Lent is a time for taking on as well as for giving up, but many adults have had to relearn what they were taught about Lent. Those who have been open to relearning a meaning of Lent would probably not choose to return to what they were originally taught.

I use this case to show that the workings of the Holy Spirit are an ongoing thing. It was not that the Church of our youth taught any of us something wrong about Lent, although we all had at least one teacher who was no more qualified to teach Sunday School than my dog is, but who got talked into it because the parish was—let's face it—desperate. It is, rather, an example of how God continually expands our knowledge and gives us new opportunities to grow and develop.

There was a day in the history of our Church—even in this century— when parishes were torn apart because the rector put candles on the altar. Imagine what might happen today if the rector did away with the altar candles in any parish. We have come to accept the symbolism of candles on the altar for what they are, but there was a time when such a change split parishes right down the middle. Not to mention the use of vestments, incense, and choirs. But God used his Holy Spirit to lead and teach men to understand all of these things. God is not stagnant. The faith is not at a standstill. The body of Christ is not dying. The Holy Spirit lives, and this is a time of great reawakening in Christendom. It is a time for the Episcopal Church to see its role as teacher and capture the moment truly for God's sake.

Today's increased awareness of the indwelling of the Holy Spirit in the lives of God's people is probably the most obvious example of the great spiritual reawakening that is going on. Speaking in tongues is not new. It didn't start in the late 1950s in Van Nuys, California, as some people believe. It started with the earliest Christians. But today we are coming to understand it as *one* of the gifts of the Holy Spirit—and not the most important one, either, I hasten to add.

But back in the late 1950s one parish in southern California was split wide open because some of the parishioners felt that some other parishioners were committing heresy by speaking in tongues. It was such a frightening experience for many Episcopalians that they decided that it must be all wrong. In another diocese, a priest received this gift and was told by his bishop not to mention it to anyone because "people wouldn't understand." Out of obedience to his bishop he did not mention it for years. To this day, there are some people, including bishops, clergy, and laity, who will not discuss speaking in tongues in any way, not even as a gift of the Holy Spirit.

On the other hand, some who have received this gift have set up just as difficult a barrier by their claims that speaking in tongues is somehow a better gift of the Holy Spirit than all others. Their gung-ho enthusiasm is so obnoxious as to close the minds of many people to discussing it, even as a gift of the Holy Spirit.

The Church—yes, the institutional Church—needs to teach its people just what the gifts of the Holy Spirit are. By their very nature, being gifts of the Holy Spirit, they must be divine; but their use can be for good or bad. The Church needs to educate its people about this very valid subject so that the workings of the Holy Spirit are known and understood by everyone, and are accepted as a natural part of God's working within the body of Christ rather than being considered just another "movement." This can come about when the institutional Church sees its role as teacher as having priority over its role as preserver of the structure.

I can envision nothing in the Church of the future that would contribute more to its healthy spiritual growth, as well as to the collateral factors of economic and numerical growth, than for it to relearn its role and see itself as the teacher of the body of Christ. When the Church begins teaching its people spiritual strengths, the economic and numerical strengths will follow. And please do not sneer at those last two strengths. They are important! Jesus has taught us that the laborer is worthy of his hire; and

Fulfilling the Body of Christ

there has to be money to pay the laborer. There must be funds to pay the Church's teachers, be they clerical or lay. Therefore, being concerned about the economic strength of the institutional Church is not to be unduly concerned about money matters.

Concern for numerical strength is not the same thing as playing the numbers game, as some people imply. Jesus told us to go out into the world and teach *all nations,* not just nice white-collar Americans with 2.4 kids and two cars. He meant for us to convert the world—not necessarily to the Episcopal Church but to Christianity. If other denominations these days are being more successful in the increase of their flocks, it may be that they are converting more people to Christianity than we are or that they are converting more people to faith in Jesus Christ than they are to membership in a particular denomination.

Because in the past the Church has not clearly seen its role as teacher, much of the teaching has come from a grass-roots level. That's not necessarily a bad thing, but it can create some problems. As the increased awareness of the working of the Holy Spirit has spread throughout the Episcopal Church, there have been people whose lives have very definitely been touched by God, whose faith has either been restored or perhaps even found for the first time. Some of these persons are among the clergy but mostly they are lay people. Since ninety-nine percent of Church membership is lay, the fact that more lay people's lives have been touched by God should not be surprising.

Lucky is the lay person whose spiritual life has been renewed and who belongs to a parish where the rector or vicar is spiritually alive. Many people are blessed with that kind of parish; but there are just as many, if not more, who do not have such an environment in which to grow.

Father Jones is often frightened "right out of his skull" when John Smith or Mary Brown walks up to him with their newfound or renewed faith and asks him if the parish can occasionally have a "charismatic" Eucharist or start a prayer and sharing group. Chances are that Father Jones has one definition of "charismatic"—John may have another, and Mary may even have a third. No word in the Christian world of the 1970s is so misunderstood as the word "charismatic." Yet where is the institutional Church on providing some teaching to the body of Christ on that one? Also, where do John or Mary go if Father Jones says No? And in a good number of parishes that is what he is saying. He is giving that response because he simply doesn't know what is involved and doesn't know where to turn to find out. Or if he is indeed open (and perhaps even grateful for the newfound or renewed faith of the Johns and Marys in his parish), he may turn to his bishop and find that his bishop may or may not know what John and Mary have been talking about.

Let's assume that Bishop Green doesn't know how to help the priest but is willing to try. Where does Bishop Green turn? To the institutional Church? To a brother bishop? To one of the organizations in the Church that are made up of committed grass-roots people? The chances are that he will receive more help from one of the unofficial grass-roots organizations or from another bishop than he will from the institutional Church.

Here I am back at the same point again: not wanting to destroy the institutional Church at all, but rather wanting the institutional Church to see the need for its increased—if not its most important—role as teacher.

Because this book is concerned with realities and visions, I have had to try to deal with the realities as I see them and share what visions I have. The reality I see is that the institutional Church needs renewal of its priorities. It needs to relearn its leadership role the same way that many of its people have had to relearn their role as Christians during Lent. The very same premise can exist for the institutional Church.

As the Body of Christ grows and deepens its commitment, there will be an ever-increasing powerhouse of faithful people—people who can be taught to share their faith with other people. Education, reeducation, continuing education, call it what you will, but whatever you call it it still centers around the need for the Church to reset its priority toward providing the teaching which its people need and for which many of its people are hungering. By education, reeducation, or continuing education, for both laity and clergy, the Church can pare away many of the extremes at both ends and can gather in its people so that they are directed toward the Lord Jesus Christ. When the institutional Church starts doing that it will find it is fulfilling the body of Christ, and it will have to worry progressively less and less about its own preservation. God will not abandon his people nor even the institutional Church which feeds and nourishes them in his name.

chapter 12

THE MINISTRY OF THE LAITY: A TEN-YEAR PROJECT

Arthur E. Zannoni

Among one of the more perplexing problems facing the Church now, and possibly in the year 1986, is the ministerial role of the laity. Unfortunately, in the Church today, the laity and the clergy are stereotyped as a result of value judgments which support a clear-cut distinction between the two. Hope for the future seems to be in an American Church which is conscious of the laity *and* the clergy, rather than the laity *versus* the clergy. Once realized, this hope would destroy the time-honored assumption "that the ministry is solely the domain of the clergy."

For the purpose of this essay, the author does not accept the distinction between the lay and ordained ministry, for as Andrew Greeley, a sociologist of religion, states: "How is the priest different than the layman? No real difference."[1] Rather than lament this previously maintained distinction, the important problem for the future is the function of the laity in the American Church.

In this year of the bicentennial, we should be aware that, unlike the Pilgrims of the Colonial days, the settlers of the untamed land, and the immigrants at the turn of the century, today's laity is technologically diversified and pluralistically educated. This makes for complicated Church assemblies. Adding to the complexity of this phenomenon is the ever-growing need to develop models for communicating the word of God to today's man in the pew. Presently, and also in the future, the man or woman in the pew may know as much or more than the man or woman in the pulpit. This does not require the Church to abandon either the preacher or the pulpit, but it does require the Church to be sensitive to the total psychic and intellectual makeup of the faithful. Outnumbering the clergy, this laity asks new questions and poses new responses, a posture that will continue in the future. This laity asks, and will ask: How do we accept the revelation of Jesus? How do we support one another in responding to the love of God that was revealed in Jesus' message?

The tentative answer is that the Church itself is a symbol of encounter and response. The Church is the locus of our encounter with God's love as revealed by Jesus and our response to that love in our own particular segment of time and space. Quite simply, the Church is the community of those who accept the message of Jesus and try to support and sustain each other in response to that message. Further, it has been and will continue to be axiomatic that the Church is constantly reforming and purifying itself.

Anyone who has taken an introductory course in sociology knows that one cannot have a community of human beings without organization, without routine patterns of behavior. The distinction that some would make between the community of the faithful as sort of an amorphous, unorganized mass, and the ecclesiastical structure as a disciplined, organized, corporate body, is meaningless. Since the community of the faithful is a human community, it will necessarily have some sort of organizational structure. The question is not so much whether we can dispense with the structure as whether the structure can be flexible enough to change as the situation changes. One group that will test the flexibility of the Church and its structures is the laity.

Commenting on this, Karl Rahner, the German theologian, investigates the positive and negative aspects of the layman's identity. He denies the historical overtones that "layman" suggests the profane, the ignorant, the nonecclesiastical, the indifferent. The layman is not the passive object of the hierarchical powers of the Church. More positively, the layman's role in the Church does not determine his role in the world, but vice versa. The specific responsibility of the layman in the world indicates his responsibility in the Church. The layman has and will have a specific place in the Church; he is and will be a member of the Church, and he exercises his function wherever the Church confronts the world and the temporal order. As no one else in the Church can, the lay person must render the grace which God invests in him historically tangible. This is the charism or grace which characterizes the function of the layman within the Church. His service to the Church is the Church's mission. However, the distinction of the layman—or better, the dedication of the layman to this responsibility and mission—must complete, not destroy, his nature as a layman.[2]

The Second Vatican Council in the Decree on the Apostolate of the Laity also makes it quite clear that the laity have an equal role in the mission of the Church. We read: "But the laity, too, share in the priestly, prophetic, and royal office of Christ and therefore have their own role to play in the mission of the whole People of God in the Church and in the world."[3]

You will notice that the Council fathers said that the laity share in the "priestly, prophetic, and royal office of Christ." Interestingly, in another document, the Decree on the Ministry and Life of Priests, it is quite clear that the laity participates in the priestly function of the Church.[4] Thus, it would seem that the conciliar fathers have established the unquestionable role of the laity in ministry.

One thing the Council did for the Church was to place it more in a communitarian than a hierarchical context. Within a communitarian context, the Church makes sense in the twentieth century; within a hierarchical context, it is a museum piece.

However, the questions before us are: What is the future of this ministry? How will this ministry be exercised over the next ten years? Will there be a uniqueness in the lay ministry that has not existed in the past? If so, what will it be?

One form of this ministry will be prophetic witness. The prophet, in the biblical sense of the term, does not foretell the future; rather, he or she reads the signs of the times in light of his or her faith, makes value judgments, and then offers some form of hope to the rest of the believing community. I think we will see the laity exercising this prophetic function with clarity and vigor in the future. They will no longer follow pious platitudes and roam dumbly as sheep. Rather, they will question their religious leaders and their own religious faith. In the future, the laity will be the conscience of the Church, just as the prophets were the conscience of ancient Israel. Any informed conscience is one that deliberates with great care before acting. For the Church to exercise its conscience, it must first be informed by the laity. Insensitivity to this conscience will lead to ecclesiastical immorality.

Further, the Church in the next decade will be equipped with a new charismatic gift. No, not speaking in tongues, but the careful, reflective process of a laity that refuses to be bulldozed by emotionalism or mesmerized by pseudo-intellectualism. As the conscience of the Church, the laity will act as both a watchdog and a sounding board for the good news that Jesus Christ is Lord.

Structurally, the Church will change. Decision-making will no longer originate in the upper echelons; it will begin in the "grass roots." Thus, the laity will exercise a greater decision-making role in the Church—not simply determining how to spend or budget money, but also engaging in theological reflection that will help the believing community the better to encounter its God. Further, the laity will not be seen as opposed to the clergy, but as being the seedbed in which the clergy take root and eventually flower.

In the future, the Church, the visible extension of Jesus Christ on earth, will survive only if it is viable to the rest of the world. Its viability stems from the living faith of the clergy and laity. This living faith caused the pagans of the past to utter: "Look how these Christians have love one for another." Will this sentiment resonate in the future? If our answer is Yes, then the Church will have to listen to the laity. Why? Because it is the laity who daily have to enthrone the cross of Christ in the marketplace, who daily encounter the demons of hedonism and religiosity. Demons change and people die, but the witness to the cross lives on in all who proclaim Christ Jesus as Lord.

Obviously, the lay person is that hand of the Church which holds the values of the temporal order; and, if the Church is destined to Christianize this world, to gather it under one head, Christ, then this hand holds the destiny and mission of the Church within its grasp. (Cf. I Cor. 12:4–31; Rom. 12:4–6).

The future of the Church does not lie in the distinction of vocations; that is, a calling to the lay life or the religious life. Rather, the future of the Church is grounded in our response to our baptismal promises and to the living out of our confirmation vows. No one has cornered the market of the Holy Spirit. The Spirit, like the wind, blows where it wills. And in the future, one place among others where it will blow and be felt is in the laity of the Church. Just possibly, the laity will help the Church's lungs to breathe in the life-giving air of the Holy Spirit.

Another function that will be exercised by the laity is that of educators. There is no longer, and possibly there will never be in the future, a lay *odium theologicum,* but rather a *fides quaerens intellectum.* Theological education, thank God, is no longer solely the enterprise or the domain of the clergy. Rather, theological education—and on the parochial level, religious education—is more a lay activity. It would seem then that in the year 2000 the Church will have more lay catechists than in the past. The next decade will contribute to populating this group. For the catechist is a man or woman taken from the people of God to proclaim the good news to all who have ears to hear; whereas a priest is a man or woman taken from the people of God to offer the sacred mysteries of the liturgy to God. Both receive their authority from God and the community; neither have authority unto themselves. For the Lord Jesus did not delegate the same authority either to his apostles or to his community that God the Father delegated to him. The command, "Go forth therefore, and make disciples of all nations. Baptize them in the name of the Father and of the Son and of the Holy Spirit. Teach them to carry out everything I have commanded

The Ministry of the Laity

you" (Matt. 28:19–20). This command was not given to a group of consecrated bishops, nor was it given to a group of ordained priests. It was given to a group of eleven or twelve laymen, social nobodies of south central Palestine, whom we refer to as the apostles. They represented the whole people of God. Further, it was a commission given by Jesus of Nazareth, a layman himself.

Another facet of the multifaceted lay witness is that the laity will exercise a greater role in determining just what the identity of the Church is, who becomes bishops, and who are ordained to the clergy, as well as how individual units of the Church are to function within the individual communities—parishes within the dioceses, dioceses within the National Church. Also, the necessity to raise the level of the consciousness of the people of God to the various needs throughout the world, whether they be ecological or psychological, will fall more on lay groups, possibly even on lay ministerial teams.

One area that seems to be emerging as unclaimed turf is the area of spirituality. With the recent upsurge in transcendental meditation, and with various searchings for ultimate meaning and meaning in life through raising the level of one's consciousness, prayer seems to be coming back into its own. The laity seem to have an insatiable thirst in the seventies, and it is my opinion that they will continue for the next ten years to drink in a viable prayer life. It seems that in the last seven years one void that the people of God have felt in their religious development is knowing how to pray. The laity seem to echo the same words as those of the apostles in the New Testament when they asked "Lord, teach us how to pray." I feel that in the next decade we will encounter groups of the laity involved in various forms of prayer, not so much with the desire of spectacular witness, such as those that some of the present day charismatics are asking for, but an increased consciousness of the power of God in their lives—more of an attempt to interiorize one's intimate relationship with God and with one's fellow man.

It may be that in 1986 the average parish will have a spiritual leader, a spiritual guru, a spiritual father, who will simply be a person who functions in a regular "secular" job, but who witnesses to a deep personal life-style and a deep prayer life that will be meaningful to many members of the parish community. It is hoped that we will all be recognized as the children of God, but not treated only as children—to be seen and not heard. Finally, the laity will attempt to dialogue with and reform the various institutions of society—political, social, economic, penal, and health. Since people change and reform institutions, the laity who staff and use these institutions are in a special position to effect redemption and salvation to all who are affected by them.[5]

The Scriptures teach us to engage ourselves in evaluation and planning, both of which in our age demand research. Not only are we told to test ourselves and our work (I Cor. 11:38; II Cor. 13:5; Gal. 6:4), but we are also to evaluate personnel (I Tim. 3:10; I John 4:1-3) and all things (I Thess. 5:21). We ought not to "judge" others in a spirit of gossip, self-righteous pride, and "holy indignation" over their faults; but we are to edify, strengthen, and stir up one another to love and to good works, helping each to find his own niche in the body of Christ (I Cor. 12:4-31), as indicated by his unique capabilities and opportunities to meet special needs. The laity will help us fulfill these scriptural mandates.

By way of conclusion, allow me to say that I trust these are fair sentiments and hopes on my part. Here I simply suggest that these are general possibilities for the future. The future will, of course, determine their viability. Such a way of setting the faith of the laity against the narrow claims characteristic of the Church calls into question the monopoly often assigned the Church and the authoritarian stance which seeks to protect that monopoly. In facing the recovery of the role of the laity as an important dimension of the Church, it will be useful to recognize some of the aspects of threat that will be felt by the Church and the clergy. Very often our understanding of ministry has been primarily informed by the assumed monopoly and its authoritarian implications. Our understanding of the mission of the Church toward the world has also been informed by this view. It is readily apparent that the protests of the laity, in the past and in the future, against this view pose a threat to every form of parochialism and every pretension of authoritarianism.

The laity do not render the Church irrelevant nor do they abolish the ordained ministry or the urgency of mission. They do raise urgent questions about the assumptions of some forms and goals the ministry and mission of the Church have when these forms and goals are not related to a concern for responsible human community.

Thus, the laity will be able to utter with the prophet Micah, and to live what was originally uttered and lived by him: "He [God] has showed you, O man, what is good, and what does the Lord require of you, but to do justice, and to love kindness, and to walk humbly with your God." (Micah 6:8).

NOTES

1. Andrew M. Greeley, *The New Agenda* (Garden City, N.Y.: Doubleday & Co., 1973). p. 300.
2. Karl Rahner, *Theological Investigation,* Vol. II (Baltimore: Helicon, 1963), pp. 318-330.
3. Vatican Council II, *Decree on the Apostolate of the Laity.* Ch. 1, No. 2.
4. The priestly function of the laity is further underscored by the Second Vati-

The Ministry of the Laity

can Council in the *Decree on the Ministry and Life of Priests,* which states: "The Lord Jesus, . . . has made his whole mystical body a sharer in the anointing of the Spirit with which he himself has been anointed. For in him all the faithful are made a holy and royal priesthood. They offer spiritual sacrifices to God through Jesus Christ, and they proclaim the perfection of him who has called them out of darkness into his marvelous light. Therefore, there is no member who does not have a part in the mission of the whole body. Rather, each one ought to hallow Jesus in his heart and bear witness to Jesus in the spirit of prophecy." (The *Decree on the Ministry and Life of Priests,* Ch. 1, No. 2.)

5. The Second Vatican Council was rather clear on the laity's apostolate to human structures and institutions when it stated: "Moreover, let the laity also by their combined efforts remedy any institutions and conditions of the world which are customarily an inducement to sin, so that all such things may be conformed to the norms of justice and may favor the practice of virtue rather than hinder it. By so doing, laymen will imbue culture and human activity with moral values. They will better prepare the field of the world for the seed of the Word of God." *(Dogmatic Constitution on the Church,* No. 36).

chapter 13

WHAT IS OUR MISSION TO YOUTH TODAY?

John W. Yates II

Youth are important! No doubt about it. The future Church will be led by the youth of today, and our mission to them today will determine the shape of tomorrow's Church. The goal of our mission has to be nothing less than our Lord's original mission for the disciples which was to "go and make disciples of all the nations." As we aim at the youth of today—those in the Church and those outside it—it must be with the goal of leading them to genuine Christian discipleship. A disciple in the New Testament sense is one who, out of a belief that Jesus of Nazareth is God's son and our Savior, and out of grateful love for him, has made a conscious decision to live out the rest of his life trusting in Christ's words and obeying his commands. Discipleship works itself out in three basic areas of relationship:

——Commitment to Jesus Christ himself.
——Commitment to the Body of Christ.
——Commitment to the work of Christ in the world.

We must develop ministries that enable youth to be committed and to grow in all three areas.

Although most of the same principles apply to grade school children, in this article I am speaking specifically of teenagers when I speak of youth. The last thirty years have shown that youth need a specialized ministry just to them. In addition to the general life of the Church, they need a person and a program aimed specifically at them. Not just anyone can work with youth. Here are some key qualities to look for in a youth worker:

What is our Mission to Youth Today?

- —He must believe in the importance of young people.
- —He must have a genuine faith in Christ of his own before he can help youth with their faith.
- —He must be in a sharing, loving, and growing relationship with at least a few Christian friends of his own age group.
- —He must be committed to his own family and see them as his top priority.
- —He does not necessarily need a seminary education, lots of experience, to be a young person himself, or to act or dress like one.
- —He must have the time to be able to be with young people.
- —He must be able to communicate with young people.
- —His desire must be to build the youth into Christ and his Body, rather than just into himself.

THE FIRST STEP

The first step in mission to youth is building a bridge to them. Some people seem to be able to relate to young people even though they may be two or three generations apart. They key is that they understand the importance of building relationships with young people. To successfully love and communicate with youth, we have to be willing to patiently work at "winning the right to be heard."

There is no way that we can build a genuinely effective youth program unless we know the kids and their needs. This means spending time with them. At Central High, playing touch football, watching drama practice, going hiking—being in their situation is the way to do this, beginning with the kids in our churches and then also moving to include their non-church friends as well. What are their names? Where do they go to school? How do they spend their time? Where do they hang out? What do they talk about? Who is interested in what? The Church must go to the youth to discern these things.

Getting together with young people "on their own turf" pays rich dividends in that:

- —You have demonstrated that you think they are important enough to talk to.
- —They are relaxed and feel secure in talking with you because they are in their own habitat. When you are first beginning to build relationships, it is far easier to have a conversation at MacDonald's than in church.
- —You've got them immediately curious simply because you're doing something probably no other church worker has done, and they want to know more about this peculiar person.

Talking with teens isn't so tough as long as we remember that they are just people and are usually shy about talking to adults until they sense we are just people too. We have to be the initiators because we are the ones building the bridge. Once it is built, then both leader and youth can communicate, but most of the work has to be done by the adults.

The idea is to center in on *them,* asking about them and their world. Honesty is a key also—kids can spot a phony a mile away. They want to know people who are real and not trying to hide anything. An adult who is not only real but is really interested in young people is a rare breed, and young people will realize what a phenomenon you are.

There are at least three reasons for taking this approach. First, it is the only way to get to really know young people. Second, it communicates to them that you care. Finally, *it is the best way to perceive needs among those with whom you are working.* But beware of accepting as fact everything young people tell you. They see things from a particular perspective which does not always give the most correct interpretation of a particular situation. Our goal is to get *into* their situation, see their perspective, then bring Christ to bear in their lives in such a way that they can see his relevance.

As you spend time with teens, seeking to get to know who they are and what they think, you discover that the typical teenager is searching for at least two things—identification and purpose. Up until this time in his life, he has been pretty much identified with his parents, but now he is beginning to move out on his own, gradually breaking away from parental ties. He wants to be free but he is not totally able to be free and is also afraid to be free because he is not yet sure of his capabilities.

Getting to know youth is like exploring a new land—you find a lot of unexpected things. I have found young people to be very, very different and yet haven't gotten to know one yet who didn't have a genuine quality of goodness and greatness down inside. Young people are great, there are no two ways about it! Many times they are selfish, immature, loud, and wild; but there is inevitably so much to them below the surface worth digging for and trying to bring out into the open, that youth work is an awesome revelation to the person who observes closely.

Even though all young people are unique individuals, there are some general needs that they all share. Let's look at some of these.

All of us and, hence, all teenagers need love. Some think of sex when they use the word love, and some think love means "never having to say you're sorry," à la *Love Story.* Many have the idea that love means approval no matter what. It is only natural that a teenager wouldn't have a mature notion of genuine love; they aren't mature people yet. But they still need mature love—they need to be loved by their peers and especially by adults. Two high school girls were talking to me after school one fall afternoon, and one complained that her strict father was never letting her out of the house on week nights. The other listened and replied tragically,

What is our Mission to Youth Today? 109

"I wish my dad cared enough about me to set some rules like that. He doesn't care where I am or what I do."

Teens also need recognition, need to be singled out and respected for who they are as they are, while not being set up as an example to the others. There are different ways to communicate recognition: a pat on the shoulder, a smile and a good word, a compliment in the presence of others, an assignment that you ask him to help you with, asking his opinion, allowing him to "do his thing" in a talent show, making a point to see him at some time other than the Sunday night meeting. You don't have to put a young person in front of the whole group to give him recognition. In fact, putting him in front of the group as some kind of example will usually put more pressure on him than is wise.

With families splitting apart, the public schools in racial uproar, and the frightening sense of international uneasiness there is no wonder that the youth of today need security. We are more and more aware of the mobile nature of our society in which every year one third of American families with husbands under thirty-five move to a new address. This keeps young people from sinking their roots in any one place and breeds insecurity, hence, the young people desparately look for security in a boyfriend or girlfriend, or in their peer group. They want to be accepted so badly that, according to a study at Purdue, 62% will go along with the crowd even if they think the crowd is wrong—so much do they fear being rejected.

Young people also have, as we all do, a real need for new experiences. Variety is the spice of life, and life can be pretty boring for Jimmy Teenager of Averageville, U.S.A. This is a basic reason why so many young people take such a wide variety of "trips" and at times seem to do such crazy things. They are just bored and looking for new experiences. If your church group can't take this need into account and come up with some new experiences, it just will not get through to a lot of needy young people.

Freedom from guilt is another basic need which all young people share. On the one hand, they have a set of principles learned from their parents and, perhaps, the Church. On the other hand, their culture operates on the surface and, according to typical teen talk, by a very different set of principles. The pressures from the crowd are so great. Virginity is "out"; the movies, the magazines, and the kids have gotten love and sex all confused. A young person who is at all physically attractive and has not had some sexual experiences is a rarity. The same is true with drugs. Marijuana is everywhere. Most kids think the laws on grass are ridiculous, but the laws are still there. For most kids cheating in school is to be expected and many teachers knowingly allow them to cheat. A major problem in many towns is burglary by teenagers—kids from wealthy homes are arrested every week for breaking and entering, larceny, etc. Some people say they do it to get money for drugs; most do it apparently just because someone else has dared them to do it and they went along so as not to be called a coward.

My point in mentioning these examples is simply that guilt builds up very easily in the heart of a teenager who has been taught one set of values at home and pushed by his peers into living, if only momentarily, by another set of principles. This guilt needs to be dealt with—the sooner the better.

Naturally, these examples are not always consistent. For example, in regard to sex, young people have a general idea that sex before marriage is a "no-no." But how many parents have ever had a serious open discussion with their son or daughter about the moral or *physical* aspects of sex? Not many would be my guess!

Teenagers have so many honest questions that they need to get answered. They need older folks who take an interest in them for their own sake and who care enough to give them the answers they themselves have come to as well as the reasons behind these answers.

Young people need to have fun. One of the great tragedies of the sixties that became a legacy in the seventies is the lack of fun and spirit among the young people. It is hard to explain until you walk around the campus of your local high school and feel it for yourself. It is a certain sense of apathy and frustration. Any youth leader needs to seek to incorporate happy, riotously funny elements into his program in order to begin to work at meeting this need. This is one of the major reasons for the great success of Christian youth ministries like Young Life—they know how to have a blast.

The fear of being inferior lurks within the hearts of almost all teenagers, and a low self-esteem is nearly a universal teen characteristic. They need desperately to know that you love them just as they are. One girl told me last week, "There's only one person in the world who really accepts me just as I am." I wish I could say that she was speaking of her parent or of me, but she wasn't. We had both failed to communicate that acceptance to her. The problem here is that sometimes, as with this particular girl, teens confuse acceptance with approval in thinking that if we disapprove of a certain action, we are not accepting them for who they are. And isn't this true even of some of us in our relationship with God? We know he does not approve of all our actions, words and thoughts, and so we fear that he does not accept us either. There is a world of difference between accepting and approving.

The other night my wife and I enjoyed a John Denver concert and sat with a teenage guy and gal who have been somewhat involved in our min-

What is our Mission to Youth Today?

istry. I couldn't help but be shocked by the real need teens have for heroes. They nearly applauded the roof right off that coliseum. Kids *do* need heroes to look up to and emulate, and we have a woeful lack of heroic material on the scene today.

Teenagers are often a bundle of contradictions. For example, they hunger for honesty—they want someone to be real with them because they are tired of phoniness. And yet the very kid who lashes out against the military-industrial war machine is a reckless driver, and the one who demonstrates for ecology turns around and disconnects his anti-pollution device to save gas on the family car. They want logical reasons for expected behavior and, yet, their reasoning is often logical only in that it is totally self-centered.

The amazing thing about teenagers is that they really are *fun* to get to know, and the rewards of becoming a friend to a teenager are endless. The beautiful thing about working with kids as a Christian worker in the Church is that so many of their real needs are met in the person of and through the body of Jesus Christ.

PROGRAM

The shape of any particular program will vary with the kids themselves and the community in which they live. The *essential* ingredients, however, must be the same as those of the New Testament Church: teaching, fellowship, worship, and outreach (Acts 2:42–47). Along with these four aspects, a fifth element must always be present: that of evangelism. We can never take for granted that our kids have accepted the faith of the fathers as their own faith. Slowly, gently, persistently, we must be presenting Christ to them in such a way that they can have their questions answered and open their own hearts to Jesus Christ in faith. Even of those who have been through confirmation, it is often true that our kids have never been brought face to face with Christ's invitation to live the new life in such a way that they have personally embraced him.

Bible study, prayer, sharing in small groups, and singing are just as important as social outings and service projects. In our last church, of the one hundred and fifty or so high schoolers involved, more than half were involved in small groups that met either before or after school in homes or at the church for a time of Bible study, conversation about their own situations, and prayer. Nearly all were involved in the weekly outreach-oriented "Breakfast in the Son" at 6:36 A.M. on Thursdays; while smaller numbers were committed to acolytes, the basketball program, and different types of service projects.

The stress must be not only on how to grow in our relationship to God but how to serve him in our relationships with the people around us. The youth group that exists purely for its own good is doomed. If our kids can commit themselves to the dual ministry of evangelism and service now, the future of the Church is an exciting prospect. But the kids cannot do it until they are evangelized themselves and taught and challenged by their scriptures.

The role of music as a unifier and medium of not only worship but also witness should be mentioned. A good music minister can involve scores of young people in choir and special productions and thus serve a major function in not only developing his gifts but in building community.

Different types of programs will attract the different types of young people. The point is, through different mediums—music, art, crafts, sports—to involve the young people in such a way that they feel a part of the whole, are drawn to Christ, and begin to utilize their gifts and pursue their interests in ways that are pleasing to God. Only the Church can perform such a ministry.

One final aspect must be mentioned—the steps of leadership. Paul's advice to Timothy was never truer than for us today: "The things you have learned from me, in turn, share with others that they may teach faithful men." (2 Timothy 2:2)

We must be leading our youth with the intention of turning over the leadership to them as they mature. Bud Wilkinson once described football as a game in which there are twenty-two people on the field desperately in need of rest yet doing *everything;* while 50,000 people in the stands desperately in need of exercise are doing *nothing.* This is too often true in the Church and its ministry. The great need today, apart from a continuing need for revival within the hearts of churchpeople, is for those who are doing the ministry well to enable others to share in the work of Christ in the world. The effective youth worker must gather around himself others who can share in the work. First, he must do the leading; then expose his "disciples" to his methods of leadership. The next step is in showing them how he does it—letting them lead while he is away in the background. In our last church we developed a youth leadership family who met with me weekly for fellowship, discussion, and planning. We worked through these stages so that when I resigned after four years, they were able to lead the work confidently and effectively.

One final word. The key is not to start big, but to start small—begin with a few young people, build into their lives, lead them to commitment and maturity, and then teach them how to reach out to their friends. Then *together* begin your larger ministry to their friends. A committed core group with a vision and a good leader can multiply one man's efforts many times over.

chapter 14

THE TRAGIC CONTINUUM AS A BASIS FOR PASTORAL THEOLOGY

William C. Spong

Jean Anouilh, the French playwright, wrote a modern adaptation of *Antigone*—a portion of the old Sophoclean trilogy. His modern *Antigone* was written in Paris within a two-year period that saw the end of World War II. The play provides a theatrical metaphor of a very perplexing human problem.

Because transparent political commentary and conversation were not permitted, many creative people, including Anouilh, took up writing. Like his mentors, Jean Cocteau and Jean Giraudoux, Anouilh sometimes turned to Greek myth for his subject matter, picking up old themes and serving them up on a modern plate, obliquely letting the chips fall where they would.

You remember the story. Oedipus, the king, was the father of the two girls, Antigone and Ismene. He also had two sons, Eteocles and Polynices. After Oedipus died, it was agreed that the two sons should share his throne, each to reign over Thebes in alternate years. But when Eteocles, the elder son, had reigned a full year and the time had come for him to step down, he refused to yield up the throne to his younger brother. There was civil war. Polynices brought up allies, six foreign princes, and in the course of the war, he and his foreigners were defeated. The two brothers fought and killed one another in single combat just outside the city walls. Now Creon (Oedipus' brother-in-law) is king, and he has issued a solemn edict that Eteocles, with whom he had sided, is to be buried with pomp and ceremony and that Polynices is to be left to rot. The vultures and the dogs are to bloat themselves on his carcass. Nobody is to go into mourning for him. No gravestone is to be set up in his memory. And above all, any person who attempts to give him religious burial will himself be put to death. Antigone, Oedipus' daughter, feels driven to bury her brother. Conflict between the law, represented by Creon, and the principle, represented by Antigone, emerges. She says, "I must bury my brother." And Creon says, "There is a law that must be obeyed. Antigone, therefore, must die." So she does. And, of course, the theme is on its way. It is tragic! The important thing is that once the tragedy begins, there is nothing you can do to stop it. It is inexorable. It moves of its own will, it is not interrupted, nor can it be.[1]

In the beginning of the play, the chorus steps out and introduces the cast. About Antigone the chorus says: "That thin little creature sitting by herself, staring straight ahead, seeing nothing, is Antigone. She is thinking. She is thinking that the instant I finish telling you who is who, and what is what, in this play, she will burst forth as a tense, sallow, willful girl, whose family would never take her seriously, and who is about to rise up alone against Creon, her uncle, the king. Another thing she is thinking is this, *she is going to die.* Antigone is young. She would much rather live than die, but there is no help for it. When your name is Antigone there is only one part you can play, and she will have to play hers through to the end. The moment the curtain went up she began to feel that inhuman forces were whirling her out of this world, snatching her away from her sister Ismene, for all of us who sit or stand here looking at her are not in the least upset ourselves, for we are not doomed to die tonight."[2] So it is that the nature of the play is that Antigone's destiny is known. That is the nature of tragedy. The chorus, when it becomes clear that everyone's fate is sealed, tries to tell the audience:

Chorus: The spring is wound up tight. It will uncoil of itself. That is what is so convenient in tragedy. The least turn of the wrist will do the job. Anything will set it going: a glance at a girl who happens to be lifting her arms to her hair as you go by; a feeling when you wake up on a fine morning that you'd like a little respect paid to you today, as if it were as easy to order as a second cup of coffee; one question too many, idly thrown out over a friendly drink—and the tragedy is on.

The rest is automatic. You don't need to lift a finger.

The machine is in perfect order; it has been oiled ever since time began, and it runs without friction. Death, treason, and sorrow are on the march; and they move in the wake of storm, of tears, of stillness. Every kind of stillness. The hush when the executioner's axe goes up at the end of the last act. The unbreathable silence when, at the beginning of the play, the two lovers, their hearts bared, their bodies naked, stand for the first time face to face in the darkened room, afraid to stir. The silence inside you when the roaring crowd acclaims the winner—so that you think of a film without a sound-track, mouths agape and no sound coming out of them, a clamor that is no more than a picture; and you, the victor, already vanquished, alone in the desert of your silence. That is tragedy. Tragedy is clean, it is restful, it is flawless. It has nothing to do with melodrama—with wicked villains, persecuted maidens, avengers, sudden revelations, and eleventh-hour repentances. Death, in a melodrama, is really horrible because it is never inevitable. The dear old father might so easily have been saved; the honest young man might so easily have brought in the police five minutes earlier.

In a tragedy, nothing is in doubt and everyone's destiny is known. That makes for tranquillity. There is a sort of fellow-feeling among characters in a tragedy: he who kills is as innocent as he who gets killed: it's all a matter of what part you are playing. Tragedy is restful; and the reason is that hope, that foul, deceitful thing, has no part in it. There isn't any hope. You're trapped. The whole sky has fallen on you, and all you can do about it is to shout.

Don't mistake me: I said "shout": I did not say groan, whimper, complain. That, you cannot do. But you can shout aloud; you can get all those things said that you never thought you'd be able to say—or never even knew you had it in you to say. And you don't say these things because it will do any good to say them: you know better than that. You say them for their own sake; you say them because you learn a lot from them.

In melodrama, you argue and struggle in the hope of escape. That is vulgar; it's practical. But in tragedy, where there is no temptation to try to escape, argument is gratuitous.[3]

Tragedy, as the inexorable movement of a person's life, is curiously juxtaposed with melodrama, which is the anxious desire of a person to raise up alternatives to the serious threats of life. There is the tragic, which cannot be altered or changed; and there is the melodramatic, which can be changed at any moment. The climate in which human pain occurs (that is, the normal human experience in which most people find themselves) is the melodramatic experience—they must find alternatives to the inexorable movement toward death. It is this curious juxtaposition (the melodramatic *vs.* the tragic) with which this paper is concerned.

I would like to suggest two ways of viewing one's life. I call these "life continuums." A continuum is a line beginning with birth and continuing through life unto death. It seems to me, as I consider the whole question of human loss—American style—that the continuum under which most people function is simplistically called a continuum of happiness. That is to say, if you draw a line from birth to death, most people would assume by definition that the continuum is described in terms of happiness, that happiness becomes the normative human experience. Happiness as normative is expected—and hurt, pain, loss or trauma are violations of that definitive, normative continuum. Man assumes that his life is meant to be happy, so that his continuum—the continuum in which happiness becomes the norm—entertains intermittent moments of pain that are violations of his defined continuum of happiness. Tragic moments within the continuum of happiness are fought and wrestled back into normalcy more often than not by the use of happiness clichés—all things work for the good. You have to look for the good in everything. God is working his purpose out. Happiness as the expected and normal part is always rejected by tragedy. So the mentality of this argument is to get everyone back into joy as fast as possible with the least trouble.

If tragedy cannot be tolerated, our loins are girded up and we swing back to accentuating the positive, eliminating the negative, latching onto the affirmative, and never messing with anything in between. According to this kind of continuum, God is seen as the keeper of the "joy gate" and guarantees a certain measure of happiness for the faithful and a divine response to good work, faithfulness, prayer, fasting, devotion. God, as the comprehensive coverer of the human experience, seems to be one that promises that the whole business of living is a business in "nonconflict," in human dignity, and in beauty. Birth to death is a continuum of happiness that has intermittent moments of tragedy which are violations of that happiness, and therefore God is seen as one who puts out gifts for people who keep their life happy and in that kind of perspective. And yet these are the kind of people who so often drive God into the wall by the presence of malignancies in their bodies, because they cannot define God as one who takes care of them on the one hand, and allows their bodies to be eaten away with carcinogenic forces on the other. It is very hard, therefore, to live under the happiness continuum and admit the presence of death-inducing disease.

The second continuum is that in which, not happiness but tragedy is seen as the norm. This is not tragedy in terms of falling down and scraping your knee, but tragedy that accepts suffering, pain, unexpected trauma, and death as the operational standard of life (as in *Antigone*), and realizes that all these things are part of the reality of existence. In this particular continuum man moves inexorably through his life toward its own conclusion, namely death. Since people in our society have such difficulty with death, the idea of it forces them into the continuum of happiness, where they even rule out the possibility that they will ever die.

Elisabeth Kübler-Ross, in her book *On Death and Dying* (New York: Macmillan, 1966), suggests that the biggest single problem American people have with dying is that deep down they don't think it will ever happen. So, as a result, they push away all kinds of preoccupation with death. But the continuum of tragedy says: I am going to live as best I can and these things are a part of it: argument, conflict, pain, hurt, death, in various patterns to be sure, but they will happen; they will happen to me and they will happen to you. It is over simplistic to say that we'll never get out of this world alive, so we might as well relax and enjoy ourselves. We're all going to die, some maybe next week; and everyone we love is going to die, some maybe tomorrow. In the continuum of happiness you cannot say that. In the continuum of tragedy you can. So instead of seeing the continuum of tragedy as morbid, what happens is that this is the only continuum where there is any possibility of admitting into one's human experience those things that one does not want to face.

When Kazantzakis has Zorba the Greek say, "Life is what you do while you're waiting to die," he is really saying something joyful. He knows that the end of life is death, he accepts it as reality and therefore he is free to live. If you function on the continuum of happiness, which defines human experience as normative happiness and in which tragedy is pushed back, then you will see Zorba's words as a depressing comment. But if you function tragically, where you move steadily toward certain conclusions that are part of being alive, then "life is what you do while you're waiting to die" becomes a revelatory statement of freedom. This freedom suggests that man accepts his life with certain destinal qualities, one of which is that there is no way we can live without dying. Death becomes a basis out of which man views his own continued human experience. In the continuum of tragedy, these tragic moments are interrupted by intermittent moments of joy, where you can reach out joyfully and participate in your world and enjoy yourself. And that enjoyment emerges because those moments are not normative.

It's really a matter of how you define things. People who have to be happy all the time are forced to translate their tragedies into happiness. Their tragedies do not have a chance to be real tragedies. Everything has to become righteous. It's like the guy who says to his wife fifteen times a day, "I love you." This casts doubts. If he says "I love you," when she is being unlovable, then she begins to realize that she gets "I love you" as a steady diet, regardless of what she says or does. The end result is that when he says it sincerely, she has long since learned to doubt the intensity or value of the feeling. It is very hard to take love seriously when its expression is a steady platter all the time.

Further, moments of joy within the tragic continuum are hallowed and beautiful because they are the fabric of the tragic style of life and are unexpected. Therefore, in the tragic style, when a person grows to expect loss, he accepts it. Freedom emerges because he no longer has to fight those inevitable moments out of his own life. He no longer has to be wiped out when he finds out he has a malignancy. He is not destroyed when he finds out that someone he loves is participating in some sort of nonsocial behavior. He does not have to go up the wall when he finds out that his kids are into drugs. He comes to experience these things, not that they would or should never happen, but that being alive invites them.

Thus, when one talks to God within this tragic category, God, as Creator, is limited by the dictates of his own creation. Man, in that dictate, is born, lives, has fun, shouts, screams, weeps, cries, suffers, and dies. That is the biblical continuum of life. There is no guarantee of finite permanence on any level. Death is an absolute reality and is preluded by sickness and those things that carry us toward death. God does not "puppet" us out of this dilemma, and anyone who insists on creating a purposive theology, as in the happiness continuum, defines God as a giant screen which is going to drop down and stop the pain that is being thrown at us, and creates a God that might ultimately be destroyed. In this perspective, there is no way that God can win. This is a God that we seize upon with the limitations of being a woman or a man, and define in such a way that if he does not live up to our definition, he has no continuance in our life. We have often created a God to worship based on what we would like it to be about instead of what it is about, and God has no chance in that theological setup except his own rejection by us. Once again, it's a curious misappropriation of definitions. When Bishop Pike was still at the Cathedral of St. John the Divine, he was giving a lecture on creation, and paraphrased Exodus 20:1-3 as: "I am the Lord thy God, thou shalt have no other gods but me, *including your best definition of me.*" It seems to me that is a significant way of understanding the problem.

We should understand the human component of this very well. Let me digress for a minute and pick up two or three problems it suggests. Consider kids in school: If you have ever been around parents of school children, you will observe that one of the interesting things they talk about is how gifted their children are. When I was in Rocky Mount, North Carolina, we tried very hard to get the public school system to open classes for the trainable retarded children. It was difficult because we found that the great majority of parents were only interested in having classes for gifted children, so they would have a place for *their* children. All parents appeared to regard their children as gifted, and this very often caused some pressing problems in the raising of these kids. One piece of fallout is that a child is raised with the understanding that his parents' happiness lies in his doing well and making top grades in school. A style emerges where an A is anticipated because he is gifted, and anything less than A is "bad" because he's "not doing his best." The result is a predefined syndrome for the child that is something like this: when he gets an A in history, he cannot really enjoy it because that is what he is supposed to do, so he has done the expected. If he gets a C, he can't enjoy that for obvious reasons, because he is not a C student. There is no satisfaction in being average. If he is defined as either failure or success, then he eliminates any possibility of enjoying either. His definitions take away both the satisfaction of notable accomplishments and the freedom to fail. He is locked into his own definition of himself learned from his parents. One's life is often controlled by the definition by which one lives. Who would have thought so much complication could come as a result of a parent being certain that he has a gifted child? It's all a matter of definition.

Another digression concerns God's rewards. If one decides that God heals the limitations and infirmities of one's life, then it might be presumed that one is defeated when there is no healing. Or one may rationalize the lack of healing by some extended spiritual resource in favor of God's ultimate knowing what is best for us. If one decides that God is going to heal the leukemic child by two hundred and fifty prayer cells all over the United States, and the child dies, then God is awful because he did not bless the life of the child. It was, you see, the predefinition that God would and could. But maybe God won't and can't! If you say "all things work together for the good of them who love God," then, when things work together for your good, you can say your faith is attributed to your good results. But if you say "all things work together for the good of them who love God," and you love God, and things do *not* work together for your good, then where are you left? That is the problem, unless you say the formula is misappropriated in the first place.

Another related problem is intercessory prayer: "O God, please heal Harry." Are we saying by intercessory prayer that its purpose is to break into the inexorable continuum of life to death and alter it? Is Lazarus still running around in space and time waiting for the death that got taken away from him? What do we mean when we say "O God, heal Harry"? Are we saying Harry should be blessed with more time on earth, or that Harry is not functioning according to the tragedy continuum? Or is it more like the young doctor who came out of the hospital room, where he had just lost the child to leukemia, and said "I cannot understand anything worse than a God who lets this child die—unless it's a God who heals him." If it became clear that God had interrupted the tragic continuum and healed this child of leukemia, then what are you going to do with that selfsame God who indiscriminately and selectively lifts up one child, while appearing to let all the other leukemic children die? Is the problem of intercessory prayer that we wish God would come in and stop what is a part of the understood created order? Is intercessory prayer an attempt to make the tragic human dimension into a happiness human dimension? Is intercessory prayer attempting to manipulate God in a way that draws credit to your life and your loved ones and your child? I think not. It is theologically and emotionally more compatible to suggest that God does not act at all—and to see that apparently hostile sentence as a statement of fact!

What about the question of the will of God? Leslie Weatherhead, when he wrote his brilliant six sermons in the London Temple during the Second World War, inquired about the child who fell off the roof and was killed on the pavement below. He asked, "Is that the will of God?" And then he said, "Yes, in that the child's body is made of bones and blood and tissue, and not Indian rubber, it is the will of God. But in that the child fell or was pushed from the roof in the first place, it is categorically not the will of God." We often hear that we must accept this or that as "the will of God," as though the death of that child, or the death of any child, or the death of any person is an individually isolated attempt on God's part to "finger" a person. "Oh, well, I don't think I have anything to do with my infinite time, so I think I'll drop a few germs on this little guy." As though God is enthroned in heaven fingering creation. "Let's have a heart attack here, or a malignancy there, a few car accidents over there." As though that's what God is about. Somehow or other, the idea that man and woman should suffer and die is a violation of something. God really should shape up and not leave us to the mute suggestion that he functions in creation according to the limitations of that creation.

One further word: many people ask: "How do you feel about spiritual healing?" Various forms of spiritual healing are being practiced in increasing numbers in the Church today, and the question is deserving of a response. My answer is that I believe in spiritual healing as long as it includes death. But when you seize upon spiritual healing as an antidote to dying, or suffering, or to what is happening or should not happen, then you may have a problem because you may be saying, "I cannot tolerate a life unto God in which these kinds of things exist." Christian theology is meaningful only when it is consistant with human suffering and loss, and that theology and suffering do not have to be ripped into polarization, so that one is Christian on one side of oneself and is running over to the other side trying to respond to losses. The Christian theology of human loss must acknowledge the *severity* of human loss, the pain of its personal and impersonal limitations, while not limiting or committing God to a dramatic or man-favoring stance.

Secondly, Christian theology must acknowledge that human loss is the obvious counterpart to human freedom and is the raw material in which man resides.

Thirdly, Christian theology affirms that death is the end of life and thus the end of man's nonresponsibility. Death is expected, unwanted, and the end of the finest gift of creation—namely, your life, which is good and beautiful and real.

Lastly, Christian theology affirms the beauty and goodness of human life as the highest act of praise. Therefore, in the words of Archibald Macleish: "We are, and what we are suffers, but what suffers, loves,"[4] and love will live out its sufferings again, endure its hardships again, rule its defeats again, and again, and again, but it still lives, and it still loves. And it is all a part of the continuum of birth to death based upon a *tragic style of life.* Human life, under a tragic continuum, moves inexorably toward its own end with intermittent moments of unanticipated joy and celebration, and is not, as under a happiness continuum, ultimately defeated by the downtrodden moments of pain.

NOTES

1. *Four Contemporary Plays.* The Modern Library (New York: Random House, Inc. 1967), p.6.
2. *Ibid.*, p.4.
3. *Ibid.*, (Re-adaptation of the Sophoclean original).
4. Archibald MacLeish, *J.B.* (Boston: Houghton Mifflin, c. 1958).

chapter 15

RELIGIOUS ORDERS: THE ORDER OF ST. BENEDICT*

Anthony Damron, O.S.B.

It is obvious that, to those of us who are old enough to remember, the world is vastly different from that in which we grew up. Many of us have seen great changes even since the day we first embraced the religious life. From all directions now come indications that there will be further changes, that there is unfortunately little contact with the past, and no way to foretell what lies ahead.

I want to suggest a twofold thesis: (1) that it is nothing less than the *confused state of the world today* which has necessitated our "renewal," our re-examination of the basic tenets of life in religion to see if that life can be simplified and returned to its primary sources; and (2) that this state of society, in producing this renewal, is providing a *saving factor* for our life and its authenticity in the modern world.

For some time now it has seemed to me that there is a false idea of permanence which exists in the religious life on several levels, and that this desire for permanence is an alien, unreligious and un-Christian spirit. When our communities, and St. Gregory's Abbey was among them, first turned from the old office books, what consternation there was in the choir! What we had was so well ordered, in our case the Monastic Breviary, the result of centuries of work! Difficult it was to leave the old books which had created saints in the past! But new insights were coming in. The Divine Office is a dialog; one hears the Word and then responds to it. There must be time to ingest the Word—to let it simmer. And then new ways might occur to us by which we could respond more genuinely and

---

*Reprinted with permission from *New Life* magazine (January 1976) vol.3,no.7.

personally. With the world rioting in the city streets, why, some asked, could not the praise of God remain stable? But the unrest crept in, made us uneasy with the kind of praise we were giving. Restyling our corporate praise in choir and adding informal worship in the way of sharing and of extemporaneous prayer were results of that unrest and enriched our life of communion with God.

We have also had to re-examine the matter of religious vows. Is it true that life vows are invariably a source of strength for one's growth in the religious life? Are they for everyone who belongs in this vocation? Or can some grow more surely into holiness without this lifelong commitment? We can see that there is a constant possibility that one may hide in his permanent vows. Initial fervor after profession dies down—we have all seen it—and the religious, even while young, levels onto a plateau. Even if the superior tries to work with the monk pastorally, he must protect the person's life vows. A religious cannot be fired, nor is he on salary. For most religious such life vows may still be viable and productive, but we must at least face the question whether they are invariably so. To be held to the religious life just on the strength that one made his vows on a certain date in the past is less than a full offering; and God may be calling him to an entirely new way of life. *Daily* commitment is what we need. We search for ways to encourage this.

The question of financial stability must be one of the most difficult problems for monasteries and convents today. Yet there should be no regret that our society no longer supports these houses as it did at one time. Essential to all religious life is the note of poverty, although that virtue is expressed in many different ways in our various houses. The economic scene, if it causes us to take a more careful look at our luxuries, many of which have taken on the guise of necessities, has done us a very fine service. At St. Gregory's, possibly for the first time, we have come through a year of minute examination of each month's expenses, if not quite with a balanced budget! One begins to wonder at that old teaching that poverty can be individual even when it is not corporate—that one can practice frugality even while the order as a corporation is affluent. No doubt this is true; one can live simply in almost any circumstances. But where is the life of faith in this when there is never any fear of hunger or cold? Wealth is not our problem at the abbey, for our securities are indeed of a modest kind. But the financial situation in the world in which we live is such that we can once again live in holy poverty, consciously offering this simple life of praise to God.

The idea of permanence has struck deep. The strength and excitement—and even the pride—which one has in his monastery or convent, the knowledge that we have worked and prayed and, as a consequence, are leaving to our future generations who will come here a house and lands and a way of life which will serve them well seems basically genuine and God-centered. And we have all wanted that. But even this is taken away, in one measure or another, from many communities. Several of our Church of England communities have had to move, no longer able to keep up the old house and grounds. Three large Trappist houses of my acquaintance are having to find new homes, squeezed out by "progress" in roadways or some other renewal. It's sad to see a convent of three old nuns, in a year's time, having to close down completely. But, again, there may be something good in this.

Is it essential for me to believe that St. Gregory's, which I love so deeply, will go on and on into the future? If in fifty years it is gone, too, will that demise lessen the power of prayer and works taking place today or in its thirty-five years of life? God may be stripping us of everything but Himself, perhaps this is the meaning of the spareness and frenzy of life today. But, if so, He is enough.

So it is that to question, and even to change such elements of our life—its prayer, our vows, our financial situation, and our permanence—may be fruitful, as I think it is. These elements are not really basically essential to the monastic life. To live according to the Gospel is the point, the whole point. And I feel that the tenor of life today has caused our religious to re-examine our convent life and to center down on that one primary purpose of it all. This is renewal, and we can thank the good Lord for sending it to us.

chapter 16

THEOLOGICAL EDUCATION IN THE NEXT DECADE

Charles L. Winters

Making predictions about the future can be a serious occupation or it can be a game. If you want to construct a highway system that will still be usable ten years from now, you should get as reliable statistics as are available about population trends, projections of auto and truck manufactures and sales, economic indicators, and even international politics. With all the data that can be obtained, projections ten years into the future are often upset by developments whose early beginnings were hidden among statistics no one thought to compile. It is a serious business. A lot of money will go into that highway system.

A late night television show, however, can feature a "fortune teller," dressed in outlandishly sequined dinner attire, who predicts a tenfold increase in the rabbit population of eastern Kansas next fall, the election of a woman President in 1988, and the rise of a Polynesian politician who will change the course of world history in 1990. The audience will laugh at the rabbit prediction, make a mental note to check the outcome of the 1988 election, and vaguely wonder about the Polynesian. It is all taken as fun and no one remembers the predictions long enough to check them for accuracy.

I am not in possession of enough data to make detailed projections which would justify the expenditure of significant capital investment in redesigned educational plants. Yet, I do not want to play games. Therefore, I shall present an admittedly subjective picture, based on some experience in seminary education, some reading of the present situation in education for ministry, and a large amount of optimism about future possibilities. I must confess to a greater confidence in the last than in the other two.

The present picture in most of our Episcopal seminaries is confusing. On the one hand, all the statistics indicate that there are more priests in the Episcopal Church now than can be hired. No matter what the reason may be, the fact is there. Yet, seminary enrollment in the last two years and the projected enrollment for next year (1976–1977) are at a very high level. Again, the reasons are not clear, but for our purposes it does not matter. Seminaries are apparently attracting people to them. In the sixties we moaned that "the best" students were staying away from seminaries in disconcerting numbers. Now they are not.

Times change rapidly. The trend in 1977–1978 may be quite different. But for the present, those of us who are engaged in theological education are experiencing encouragement that is very heady indeed. Since I do not believe that panic is a good state of mind in which to take stock of one's enterprise, the corollary would seem to be that the present situation presents an admirable opportunity to do just that.

The first pair of questions which comes to my mind as I begin the stocktaking are: How good a job are the seminaries doing? And what are they doing it for? These are not isolated questions. They imply a further pair: Can we do the job better? And ought we to modify our goals?

How good a job are the seminaries doing? The answer to that really depends on how one answers the second question—that of the goals. Not very long ago, the generally accepted expectation was that seminaries would produce men (not women!) who were cast from the mold of the scholarly English country parson, able to read their Scriptures in Greek, quote from the ancient fathers, preach erudite if not terribly inspiring sermons, know their parishioners well and be on hand to help them over times of crisis. This is not at all a bad set of expectations (except for the sermons, and in their case it was probably more a concession to reality than a true expectation).

But many circumstances have conspired to make these expectations no longer generally realizable. Most students do not come to seminary possessing a knowledge of the Greek language, and there is not enough time in seminary both to learn the language and to use it in the study of the New Testament. One must use "helps" for this until about the last year of seminary, by which time the New Testament has been covered. Besides this, the world has become so much more complex than the one that the "scholarly English country parson" lived in that many new disciplines have been crammed into the typical seminary curriculum, crowding out some of the time spent with the ancient fathers. And it does not seem possible these days to find a community which is stable enough for the parson to solemnize the wedding of the boy and girl he baptized.

The seminaries can rightly claim, however, that they are succeeding in helping people who entered seminary, with considerable faith but rather little knowledge, to develop a Christian maturity which should stand them well in future years, whatever form their life of service may take. *Simple* faith is good; *simplistic* faith is not likely to stand the tests of life. While some students hold to their simplistic answers from fear of losing their faith, by far the greater majority survive the anguish of learning and graduate with a faith that is deeper and more secure than the one with which they began. To me, this means that the seminaries are doing a fairly good job.

In addition to this, seminaries are introducing their students to a fairly sophisticated level of competence in a wide range of skills which were largely unheard of a few decades ago. The sciences of psychology, anthropology, and sociology are providing insights into the profession of ministry which allow newly graduated seminarians to function in ways that years of experience have not succeeded in producing in the past.

All is not rosy, however. To see the problems, we must turn to the second question: What are they doing it for? Here, some serious confusion exists. I am prepared to grant (simply because I do not care to pursue the question) that a time may have existed when a three-year period of seminary instruction was sufficient to provide all the training necessary for a life of ministry. If so, it prevails no longer. The continually changing demands of modern society cannot be anticipated adequately enough to design training to meet them, and three years does not give sufficient time even if they could. If seminary education is expected to meet this goal, it must inevitably fail.

Before considering the further implicit questions—Can we do the job better? Ought we to modify our goals?—let us turn to another dimension of the Church's ministry to which the seminaries have only tangentially addressed themselves: the ministry of the laity. Christian theology has always taught that every member of the Church is called to ministry by virtue of his or her baptism. This notion, which is unimpeachable from the standpoint of biblical and theological teaching, has been preached again and again, but little has been done to enable it to bear fruit.

When a faithful member of the Church takes seriously the exhortation contained in countless sermons to take up the ministry of the laity, he or she is greeted by a confusing set of responses. At first, a series of "jobs" in the Church are offered, each one fully meritorious, even essential. The Church needs people to serve on the vestry, to teach Sunday School, to be lay readers or chalice bearers. Work with youth is always sufficiently challenging to need a supply of replacements. Organizations for all sorts of worthwhile community projects need people to work in them. All of these functions are good and important, and they do indeed constitute some aspects of lay ministry. The trouble is twofold: they either do not require very many people to do them, or only with difficulty can they be seen as constituting *Christian* ministry.

That is to say on the one hand, that the specifically churchly functions consist of what is in reality staff work—the teaching staff, the liturgical staff, the youth workers staff—or board work, the vestry. This leaves most of the parishioners out. May God continually call people to these positions, for the Church could not function without them; but lay ministry must include more than this if it is to embrace all baptized persons.

The other problem lies in the fact that good works done in the community seem to many people to qualify as Christian ministry only when and because they are sponsored by Church organizations. The work itself could be done by countless other charitable organizations. If a person senses a call to Christian lay ministry, such work may not seem to suffice.

There is still a third response that is made to lay persons who seek a significant ministry: they can witness to the Gospel of redemption in their everyday lives. Many a lay person who hears this response goes away sorrowing, not because the response is inadequate, but because they feel inadequate to the task.

This, I believe, is the crux of the matter. *Lay ministry requires theological education just as much as ordained ministry does.* When a priest preaches the Gospel from the pulpit, he does so out of the background of the best theological education the Church can provide. Why does a lay person need less to do the more difficult job of interpreting the significance of Jesus Christ in the concrete settings of life? Simple faith, even in simplistic form, can indeed reach into the hearts of some people. But simplistic slogans are an affront to many more. Episcopalians, for better or for worse, do not like to be a cause of affront. It is not necessarily a sign of weak faith for a person to say, "I can't do that." It is more probably a simple statement that the person does not feel properly equipped.

Somewhere in the total picture of theological education, then, serious, systematic, and sustained education for the ministry of the laity must find a place.

Now, to return to the questions of whether or not the job of theological education can be done better, and whether or not the goals should be modified. As I see it, the key to the first question lies in the second. The goals should be modified considerably. First, the three-year seminary curriculum should be expected to achieve much more modest goals than those currently set for it; second, the goal of theological education as such should be expanded to include the laity; third, new goals should be set for the continuing education of both clergy and laity throughout their entire ministry.

THE SEMINARY CURRICULUM

Too much has been expected of seminaries. A basic introduction to the Bible and the Christian tradition is a realistic goal. Specialized, in-depth study of one, or even several, areas within the corpus of this biblical-historical tradition is also possible. Training in professional competencies over a fairly wide range can be done. Assimilation of the Christian heritage into one's life, so that one's attitudes and ministerial style begin to be reshaped and one's relation to God and one's vocation begins to take on some degree of clarity—this, too, is not an unrealistic goal. But all of them together are not possible!

If the initial three-year seminary program is expected only to *begin* the process of ministerial education, those goals which can be best met within the allotted time can be selected, and the others assigned to other times, and perhaps other agencies. I think that the first and the last of the above mentioned goals are the most appropriate: introduction to the biblical and historical tradition, and assimilation of this for personal transformation and role identification.

I expect the cry to go up that this means a lowering of academic standards. It need mean nothing of the sort. A far higher level of achievement is reached when important issues are understood in such a way that one's attitudes and actions are changed than when mountains of disconnected data are accumulated. Clear and achievable goals lead to better education than attempts to "cover" the whole range of available knowledge.

This is not to imply that opportunities for students to explore the issues their core study raises should be withheld. Nor is it to suggest that training in the rudiments of professional competence should be neglected. It is to maintain, however, that these are to be done in a manner and to a degree that is consonant with the primary goals of immersion in the tradition for the formation of ministerial style and identity. Seminaries cannot produce "well-rounded priests," but they can and should graduate people who are solidly grounded in their faith and who know who they are in their vocation.

LAY THEOLOGICAL EDUCATION

The ministry of the laity cannot achieve its full potential until (a) it is more clearly identified, and (b) it is trained. The distinction between "staff" ministry and some other less well-defined kinds has been suggested above. Let us explore the distinction further. Any institution needs to have various tasks done *in order for it to continue in operation*. The Church, as an institution, must be maintained in its operation. It must make sure that its tradition is handed on from generation to generation. It must see to the admission of new members. It must gather together to hear the Word of God from which it lives, and to give worship to God. It must be provided with leadership, with teaching, and with counsel. It must mediate authoritatively to its members the gracious and enabling power of God. All these are ministries *to the Church*. They are appropriately done by those ordained specifically to this function. Laity, of course, can *assist*—and their assistance is invaluable. But the major responsibility for these "staff" or maintenance functions rests with the clergy, and the Church should rightly require long training and accountability to undergird the authority with which it invests the clergy.

But when all these functions have been accomplished, the Church still merely exists; its own ministerial role has not yet been fulfilled. Two further kinds of ministries must be done: the Christian Gospel must be *practiced* and the world must be *evangelized*.

To speak of the "*practice*" of the Gospel implies both nuances of the word: it means the continual attempts to live out the Gospel, with corrections and renewed attempts and the development of greater ability; and it means the formation of life-styles, individual and corporate, that more nearly reflect the values of the Gospel. This is "practice" in the sense of training. At the same time, it means the day-by-day life itself, lived as a response to the good news. One practices in order to learn, and one puts into practice what one has learned.

The practice of the Gospel is, therefore, the whole life of the Church. But for it to become a reality, *someone must do it*. The people of God are called to this; the *laity* (the word itself means "the people") have this as their baptismal vocation. This ministry, the ministry which is done *within* the Church, is not simply "living a good life." It involves the ability to discern the manifold calls from God which are mediated by the lives of our neighbors; the ability to discern those responses to one's neighbor which are redemptive and fulfilling; and the ability to do these things as ministers of redemption and reconciliation. It involves the critical faculties of evaluation and reflection by which the word of judgment comes into one's life with its call for change and redirection. In short, it involves the same immersion in the biblical and historical tradition and the formation of a ministerial style and identity which is necessary for the ordained ministry.

Evangelism, a word spoiled by its too close identification with nineteenth-century revivalism, means "gospeling": declaring the good news to the world. This is done in countless ways, of which preaching to large groups of people is only one, and by far the least effective. The more difficult but more effective ways include the day-by-day manifestation of love, joy, and peace; the life of servanthood to stranger and enemy as well as friend; interpretation of life to a secular age so that it begins to make sense and discover its purpose; opposition to hatred, war, and oppression in the name of Jesus. These and other acts in which Christian people bring the good news to the world comprise the ministry of evangelism.

The same immersion in the biblical and historical tradition and formation of ministerial style and identity is required for this ministry. And this ministry can only be done by *the laity*, because it must be done throughout the world—that is throughout *all the areas of human life*. The people of God, the laity, live in all these areas, and they are the evangelists. They "bring news," as all people do, by their actions and words. The only question is whether the news they declare is the good news or something else.

Thus, the ministry of reconciliation and redemption and the apostolate of evangelism are the vocations of the laity. Clergy are called to them too, of course, but in their *baptism*, not in their ordination alone. Sustained and systematic theological education for the laity is essential if these ministries are to be fulfilled. The little disconnected snippets of information that have been doled out in adult education classes will not do. Considerable commitment of time and energy will be required, but in many ways the laity of the Church has been saying for years that *it is willing to make this commitment*.

CONTINUING EDUCATION FOR CLERGY AND LAITY

Limiting the goals of the three-year seminary to what is necessary for a *beginning* of ministry requires as its corollary that the other essential dimensions of theological education be provided at later times. The Church must make some radical revisions of its ways of doing things if this is to come about.

Clergy and laity alike need specialized training as well as the grounding provided by their initial theological education. The Church, for example, must have a continuing supply of persons whose vocation is to theological scholarship. Means for pursuing graduate education, therefore, are needed. There is no such thing any longer as ministerial competence: there are manifold ministerial competencies, and continued means for acquiring and maintaining these competencies must be provided.

This means much more than simply having training programs *available*. The *means* must be provided by which to engage in them, and the Church should *expect* such continuing education as a normal part of ministry, for which one is held *accountable*. This requires a new financial structure and a new deployment procedure. The Church can no longer coast on the assumption that a one-day, loose-change offering on Theological Education Sunday will suffice to finance the training of its ministry. The Episcopal Church is timid in asking its members to be faithful stewards, but the time has come when each parish must be asked to accept its responsibility for Christian ministry.

By the same token, the ordained ministry must come to accept its accountability to the Church. Seminary students are held accountable throughout their three years, but upon ordination accountability ceases. Evaluation, continuing education, and continuing expectations are essential for a ministry which can keep pace with the changes of the modern world.

If this three-fold vision of a pattern for theological education in the future comes to pass in any significant degree, there will be enough work to occupy all of our seminaries and still require assistance. Not too long ago it was being urged that most of our seminaries be phased out as uneconomical and redundant. At the present time they remain costly and are still redundant—but they are needed for the future. The cost, I am afraid, is inevitable. From a financial standpoint, consolidation into large institutions may be more efficient (though probably only slightly so), but the very purpose of a seminary is defeated if the educational process is dehumanized in the name of efficiency. There is no substitute for small, intimate groups of learners working in close relationship to their faculty if the processes of immersion and formation are to take place. Information delivery, of course, can be done in large economy packages—but education for ministry cannot.

Redundancy, however, is avoidable. Our seminaries have differing gifts and resources. Their traditions, faculties, locations, and connections with other institutions make them better able to do some things than others. Some are not at all equipped to offer graduate-level education, while others are admirably so. Some are more closely related to typical parish life than others. In the broad range of theological education as suggested here, encompassing not only the three years of preparation for ordination but also the entire range of lay and continuing education, stock should be taken of our seminaries and the areas of specialization developed among them.

But beyond this, a relatively new phenomenon in theological education is developing: dioceses are training people for ministry within their own jurisdictions, using their own personnel. What is new about this is not the fact itself, but the explosion in the numbers of them. A report about to be published will show an amazingly high percentage of clergy being trained in such diocesan programs.

The seminaries have deplored this. They see an inevitable lowering of the educational standards of the clergy as the result. I think this evaluation is both true and irrelevant. By no stretch of the imagination could it be supposed that either scholarship or pedagogical competence are equal between full-time and part-time educators. Instances can be found of brilliantly competent scholars and teachers among parish clergy and of dullards on seminary faculties, but policy cannot be made on the basis of exceptions. Yet, granting this, the diocesan programs exist *because they are needed*. Most of those responsible for their development are aware of the dangers to quality which they present; some have asked repeatedly for help from the seminaries to avoid this.

An alliance between seminaries and diocesan part-time theological education programs makes so much sense to me that I cannot believe it will be forever denied. Most of lay theological education, much of continuing education, and some training for nonstipendiary ordained ministry can be done best at the diocesan level. If the seminaries will provide resources and guidance—perhaps educational modules for local implementation—the alliance will mean better theological education throughout the Church.

I am optimistic enough to think something like what I have suggested can happen. Some, disputing my theses (for which, as I admitted at the outset, I claim no exhaustive sets of data), may not regard this as optimism at all. But if not these patterns, then some equally radical changes in our notions of theological education are not only necessary but in the process of incubation. The next decade should be a good one for theological education.

PART III

The Church in Society

chapter 17

AN AMERICAN INDIAN VIEWPOINT

Marllene Campbell

"Stir up, we beseech thee, O Lord, the wills of thy faithful people; that they, plenteously bringing forth the fruit of good works, may by thee be plenteously rewarded." These famous words from the Book of Common Prayer have been said many times but nothing has really been done about them.

In my travels I have noticed that the Church needs to be stirred up to where the people will really come to understand the true meaning of being a Christian. There are entirely too many Sunday worshipers; they go to church on Sunday and lose all spiritual feeling on Monday. And there are people who go to church for the sake of attending and not for the sake of the true meaning; socially, it is good to be seen in church with the family. There are also people who attend because they think their children—not themselves—need this direction in their lives. I am sure this is happening all over the world, not just with the church I attend or the diocese in which I live.

I know there are well-planned programs in parishes and missions throughout the nation that are available to the congregations if they desire them. But how does one become involved with people who are not really interested? It seems that the programs are set up only for the people who are already interested in parish work and are attending church regularly. I strongly believe that the Church is not really doing what it should be doing for the people we call "lost." I don't care for this word, but I suppose it is the only word to describe the people of whom I intend to speak.

I would like to open my subject with the problems that currently exist on our Indian Reservations. It would seem that with the strong assistance of the Church in this area these problems could be solved to some degree. Of course, a complete resolution of the problems of the American Indian would be impossible, at least for the near future.

In the year 1873, Bishop Hobart Hare came to what was then the Dakota Territory. With very little assistance and a giant heart he was able to convert a great many of our Indian people to Christianity. He was a small man but powerful and courageous. The Indian people slowly opened up to him, finally giving him their wholehearted respect. This happened in the years when the Christian missionary was tough, mentally and physically, and when the Church rules were strict.

There was a time when the churches on Indian Reservations taught that it was a great sin for any church leader to take part in any kind of celebration conducted by the Indian people. This was because such things harked back to their pagan past or had contributed to the disintegration of the Indian people. Church leaders were treated with great respect because they never involved themselves with dancing (Indian or other), social drinking, Indian gambling games, or anything else that could cause or lead to some kind of sin. Today the Church has changed and many restrictions have been lifted. Church leaders have lost the great respect they once had, and because of this the membership is dwindling.

I am concerned for the future of the Church because, even if there were no God, the Church, with its teachings of good and evil, has helped in such problems as crime, alcoholism, suicide, neglected children, broken homes, divorces, hatred, and others. It has taught love and respect for one another, and this alone has helped all the other bad situations on our reservations.

As I see it, the Church must regain its leadership in providing that great and necessary help to our Indian people who are home on the reservations, not from choice but because of unsatisfactory situations. A great effort is needed to organize for this task, as well as for the budgeting of sufficient funds.

Rebuilding our native people in Christianity would be a giant project that would have to begin from the beginning once again. Powerful missionaries would have to be sent to the reservations to attempt to put back the love that is lost in many family households between brother and brother, sister and sister, father and son, mother and daughter. This is where it would all begin, within the nuclear family; but the problem is much larger than that. In some cases there is a bad relationship between families in community and between families on a reservation. Even on a yet wider basis, there are bad relationships between bands of Indian people within a whole tribe, not to mention friction between tribes. These intertribal conflicts seemed to be settling down until a few years ago, but lately they seemed to flare up again.

As if this were not enough, I feel that the most significant rupture in relations is that between the Indian and the white man. This also was improving until a few years ago, and then it began to deteriorate. Reconciliation is the Church's primary task, and I believe it has its work cut out for the next ten years or longer.

The Church speaks of self-determination among our Indian people, and our own Indian leaders agree. They speak of it as one way of attempting to solve some of the present problems existing on our reservations. Self-determination is not yet a fact, however. One way of achieving it, we are told, is through nonstipendiary clergy. This may work in some areas and with some priests, but on our reservations it seems to mean being a priest who is only half willing to serve the Church, or who is serving two masters. The Indian has always been taught that this was not possible for one working in the Church.

It has been known, accepted, and respected for many years among our Indian people that the place of the clergyman was with his people, fully and wholeheartedly. This thinking goes further back and has a certain identity with the Medicine Man. He did not have to do anything except keep his people comfortable spiritually. His job was not a part-time job; it was for always and it began when he was a child, not after he had grown and had become an adult person.

To be self-determined and to uphold our own churches on the reservations may be a wonderful idea for some. It would take away much of the Church's responsibilities and headaches in the missionary field. The great problem, however, remains: to educate Indian leaders for this self-determination we are trying to achieve; but even if we succeeded, many of the future Indian clergy would have to work without pay. This, I think, is ridiculous. I ask myself many times: Why, when the people are giving to the Church for the support of priests elsewhere, should not this include our Indian people?

If our full intentions are to improve our Church's programs and rebuild its structure, we must restore the love and joy that was taught and experienced by the Church. This will also require a new beginning. We cannot build a new structure on an old foundation. We have to rebuild the foundation first of all.

Another thing that is always a tangle in my hair is the communications media. Why is it that when something happens on our reservations that has to do with welfare or starvation, death or murder, it always seems to make the front pages or the radio and television newscasts? Yet when the Indians are witnessing to their unity in God it goes unnoticed. I would like to relate one such incident in this area. In the spring of 1975 our Indian people were having what is called their annual Niobrara Convocation on one of the reservations, and at the same time a small group of militants were having a bout with the law in another area of the same reservation. The few militants received national attention, but the two thousand Indians and visitors who were worshiping God and having a joyous time for three days were never mentioned at all. I think that national recognition should occasionally be given to the Christian Indian. This always seems to help stimulate the work of the Indian people and the missionaries. I realize that part of this task is the responsibility of people like myself and the Indian people around me, but we are not experienced journalists or photographers. This may seem like a little thing, but it would mean so much and would encourage church activity among our Indian people.

There are many programs that would be helpful to our young people, and I think the Episcopal Church should undertake them. First of all there is the education of the children. I realize that our clergy and church workers on the reservations have this responsibility, but they can only go as far as their financial reserves will allow. They can handle Vacation Bible School and, in some cases where adults are willing, Sunday School. But the great need is to train teachers so they will feel confident in teaching the Bible to children. This usually involves expensive and extensive workshops, which are not always possible on the reservations.

The Roman Catholics have numerous schools set up on our reservations that educate the Indian children from the kindergarten age to and through high school. The Episcopal Church in the Diocese of South Dakota has one school for Indian girls, which is of excellent quality; but there are only fifty girls enrolled at the present time. There is also an Episcopal Boys Home, which seems to be going downhill because of the lack of attendance and a shortage of finances; there are only fifteen boys now enrolled in this home. Why couldn't the Church help to expand these two institutions to make them more attractive to the people, especially to the parents of Indian children? This would be a great help to our less fortunate Indian Christians, and our goal of self-determination could become a reality.

In this paper, such things as the Green Book, the Zebra Book, the new Blue Book should probably not be considered serious issues. I feel, however, that if I am to tell my true feelings and that of my Indian people, they should be discussed here because they involve much controversy among the Indian leaders in the Church.

Our Indian people have, and have had for many years, a prayer book all their own. Drawn from the Book of Common Prayer, it is bilingual and contains all the important services, those that are most constantly used by

An American Indian Viewpoint

the people. Our people feel that they should not have to put away this wonderful book and replace it with one they do not really understand. Our present book, which is almost a hundred years old and is a great treasure and comfort to us, would have to be retranslated. I think the future of the Church on Indian reservations would be more secure if it held on to the Book of Common Prayer.

Indian people are also concerned for the future with regard to the possibility of women priests. In the ancient Indian culture there was always a Medicine Man but never a Medicine Woman. It is an idea that the Indian finds hard to accept. The woman lay reader is accepted in many areas because of the choice and character of the person. Some of the Indian women feel that, even though they might be lay readers, they would not feel right in the position of priest. Perhaps, given a few years, their attitude may change; but at present the majority is strongly opposed to having women priests.

The future of the Church is really in the hands of the youth of the Church. Much will depend on the training and development of young people. I am speaking of our teenagers, the age group that seems to be most troubled about their relationship with the Church. The search for identity plays an important part with young people, and I am persuaded that the teenager of today can be helped to achieve identity and a satisfying and beneficial future. Yet, while we have young people who are true Christians and who fully understand what the whole Church is all about, there are many who are hiding in the shadows and pointing fingers at the "goody-goody" kids. Perhaps they are really envious of those who are having all the fun and joy of Christian love and togetherness. But how are we to reach them?

The Church operates beautiful camps which are being used by both the young people and the adults. But there are many young people who will never know the great joy and satisfaction that can come from such camps, and my concern lies with them. The Church should make a great effort to reach our youth in every area. We must cooperate wherever possible with different denominations which are interested in this endeavor. Ecumenism is a great movement and should begin with the young people. In many areas it probably has. Indian youth could benefit by knowing and understanding their own culture better, as well as that of other ethnic groups. This is possible in some of our schools, but not in the Church. Why? It would be interesting, for example, to know why certain people, including the Indian people, have particular traditional foods, and how this fact represents or embodies their sense of identity. Such sharing of cultural differences would be a great help in bringing the people closer together in their attempts to understand one another.

It worries me when I think of the thousands of young Americans who have left their homes and schools to join evangelical crusades—the Children of God, the Jesus People, the Divine Light Mission, and other lesser-known sects. I feel that the Episcopal Church should be in there somewhere heading a crusade for Christ and bringing in the young of our denomination. In the near future perhaps this will come about.

What I have to say in conclusion may not be what the Church will see as necessary to its mission; but I think it should be mentioned.

There are Indian people who are successful farmers, ranchers, auto mechanics, and such, and they are doing fine in making an attempt to care for themselves. There are also those who are living off the reservation and are making the same attempt. But there are far too many who are living by handouts from the federal government—Aid to Dependent Children, Social Welfare, Old Age Assistance, food stamps. I feel that if we as Indian people ever intend to be completely on our own, then we are going to have to find a way to free ourselves from the handouts. Many of our people think that the government owes this to us. But it is certainly not helping us to be responsible for ourselves or to gain a sense of our own dignity as Indians. Some of us are tired of having our people continually living out of the white man's billfold.

Self-determination is not, and should not be, the sole concern of the Church. It should also be a priority of the federal government. If our people are going to improve themselves, they are going to have to do it on their own. I believe the Church could be of great help here, not by giving money but by giving us the education to plan our own future. I realize that we are in need of money, and that it takes money to run a successful program. The Church has helped countries all over the world with programs and personnel and by teaching the Word of God. This is good and should be carried on in the future. But we should also look around in our own house and see what's troubling the people sitting there in the corner. What has recently brought this to my attention is a report concerning world hunger, which stated that as we see people in other countries starving and begging for food, we need to remember that there are 9,000 people, mostly Indians, in our own state of South Dakota who are starving or ill because of malnutrition. How many other states in our country are there where people, largely minority groups, are going hungry and the Church is not even aware of it?

I look to the future of the Episcopal Church as being a busy and successful one. I feel that evangelism is very important because it will help recruit members to our ranks, and we need to build our membership. Christian education and leadership training are also important and should be broadened in the future. A youth program is another great need. Every

An American Indian Viewpoint 143

diocese should employ a youth director who is a recognized leader in the diocesan family. If this is impossible, as it is in some dioceses, the National Church should see to it that each diocese receives the necessary help in hiring a qualified youth director. More than anything else, I think the future of the Church lies, finally, in what we do about our young people.

chapter 18

THE ROLE OF THE URBAN CHURCH: ITS PROBLEMS AND OPPORTUNITIES

Paul Moore, Jr.

Twelve years ago, I wrote a book called *The Church Reclaims the City*. Although the title is not mine, it reflects at least a modicum of optimism on the part of Church people and people in general as they looked at the modern city at that time. In contrast, last Sunday I preached an Easter sermon which stated that New York and other great cities are dying. We are now far beyond the life or death of the Church in the city, we are now wondering about the life and death of the city itself, and, in turn, the survival of our very civilization as we know it, because historically, the cities have been the souls of their nations. Babylon, Alexandria, Jerusalem, Athens, Rome, Paris, London, New York, all symbolize the culture and power of the particular nation of which they have been the flowering. One cannot conceive of a civilization and a culture without a city, although some sociologists today say that the city is an outmoded political, economic, and institutional form. A recent editorial from the periodical *Urbia* states it this way:

The City is a state of mind. Whether our cities will survive into the year 2000 depends on whether we can maintain that state of mind. There are strong indicators that the answer is no. The city man is characterized by a Freudian personality, motivated by the Protestant Work Ethic and ruled by scientific reason. In all these traits, he differs from feudal man, who preceded him, and corporate man, who supersedes him. For the archetypal incarnations of city man, business man, industrialist, politician, citizen, the future is a shrinking arena. For their inheritors—bureaucrat, manager, advisor, corporation functionary—there is expanding opportunity, but in a life style that no generation of the past would recognize as human.

Whether or not this prophecy is true, I believe that the major vocation of the Church of God in the United States is to address the problem of the disintegration of the cities of our land. Cities are directly related to every human being who lives in the United States, every human being who has a television, every human being who is linked one way or another with the federal government; which is linked, in turn, with the great urban centers of our country. New York flounders because refugees have come to New York from the Caribbean, from the rural South, from all the areas of the world where survival was not possible. Historically, New York has nurtured and educated immigrants and sent them forth into the mainstream of American life, building up the very bones and body of our nation. Today, for many extremely complex reasons, New York is no longer able economically to carry out this function. And if New York dies, Chicago will die, Yonkers will die, San Francisco will die, and someday even the cities of the new, sunny Southwest will die. When I say "cities" I am not speaking just of a place where there's very little grass and a lot of buildings, but I am speaking of a center of commerce, industry, and culture. I speak of a place to which the great mix of humanity finds itself attracted for the need to survive or the need to conquer. The glory of the city is the vitality which millions of people living in close proximity bring to the creative ventures of our civilization; the agony of the city is the thousands upon thousands of poor people and minority people who are disintegrating in mind and body and soul because of the short-term economic and political decisions of our land.

With that very brief, surrealistic description of the present city, let us look back at some of the modes of mission that the urban Church has employed in recent years.

At the turn of the century the so-called "social gospel" led the prosperous churches of the city to establish settlement houses or chapels for the poor in the less fortunate parts of town. There were German-speaking, Italian-speaking, even Polish-speaking missions. There were missions addressing the needs of black persons and, later, persons of Spanish background; there were missions in Chinatown in San Francisco and in New York. The theology of this pattern was based on the nineteenth-century *noblesse oblige*—not a bad theology as far as it goes—whereby those who had much had an obligation to share with those who had little. Naturally, there was a degree of paternalism in this kind of mission, because the rich churches maintained control over the policy and personnel of the work. About the time of World War II many mainline Protestant Churches were leaving the cities because their constituents had moved elsewhere. Even some of the new immigrant groups had gone to greener pastures. So there was a new series of movements to bring the mission of the Church to the postwar city. These movements were working against the flight to the suburbs, which was greater then than at any other time before or since, because the policy of the federal government made it easy to build in the suburbs and hard to build in the city. Some of these movements in our Church were the Society for the Promotion of Industrial Mission, the Urban Priests Group, the Episcopal Urban Fellowship, the Division of Urban Industrial Work at the National Council (Executive Council), as well as particular communities of clergy and laymen establishing new methods to reach the city.

One of the principles of the Urban Priests Group, with which I was associated, was to bring the altar and social action and social service together. We had been inspired by the priest-worker movement in France and by the so-called "slum priests" of the early twentieth-century Oxford Movement in London. We felt deeply that the Church's ministry must be one—that the altar, the hospital, and the jail could not be separated. The financing of these works came from national and diocesan sources or from parish endowments. There was an excitement and romanticism in the air as we tried to emulate Dorothy Day of the Catholic Worker Movement and St. Francis of Assisi.

In the sixties things began to change. The Civil Rights Movement gathered momentum and drew many urban, concerned churchmen to its national level. The government began the Anti-Poverty Program and asked the Churches to host government-subsidized programs, with the *caveat* that these could not be used in any way as sources of evangelism. Harvey Cox, in *The Secular City* (New York: Macmillan, 1966) undergirded the movement with his theology, which could be simplisticly stated as saying "the Kingdom of God and the Secular City are one." This movement ran its course, and the Churches could take pride in volunteering their facilities for secular programs. But now, as the secular programs have dwindled to almost nothing, we are left with empty churches, no urban strategy, and precious little financing to carry out our mission. In the Diocese of New York alone we have fifty inner-city parishes; inflation and shrinking endowments make it almost impossible to give them the resources they need to minister to their neighborhoods. Our first priority is the presence of the Church in poverty communities, and yet each year we are less able to make that presence effective. Thus it is a time of discouragement for many of us, for we had dreamed in the early seventies that the Church could be a strong force in reconciliation and unification after the racial trauma of the sixties—a humanizing influence upon the dehumanized communities of the modern city.

The Role of the Urban Church: Its Problems and Opportunities

Where do we go from here? It is hard to say. We seek the guidance of the Holy Spirit daily to give us a clue as to where to go. We keep watching and waiting and listening for the signs of some new movement rising from the streets and the parish churches to catch us up in its excitement and enthusiasm. I long for the day when the deep wounds between black and white can be healed and once more we can go forward together as peers with new mutual respect. I look forward to the day when the Church will no longer be racist and sexist, because the struggle that lies ahead cannot afford a Church lacking in integrity in any aspect of its life and work.

We wonder what we can do about the great and glorious landmark church buildings in the old cities of the country which symbolize the presence and continuity of the Church of older generations. Is it God's will, so to speak, that these sacramental evidences of this presence should be destroyed? Are we to go out on the street once more and begin from scratch and let these great buildings fall down? These are the questions that face every urban diocese and, in turn, face the National Church. What are our priorities for the Gospel? Can we carelessly close the great churches which so many generations have built, and which give the changing city a sense of permanence, of hope, and of spiritual presence? These are terrible decisions, and yet there they are, staring at us, becoming more crucial every day.

I do not know the answers, but I do see some hope and renewed life which may be signs of the future. There is a renewed interest on the part of many young people in the Christian faith, not a passing or exotic interest but a vocation to roll up their sleeves and work for the kingdom in whatever way they are called. In the Diocese of New York alone, there are over eighty-five nonstipendiary clergy, and many more are joining their ranks each day. We are trying to learn to deploy this renewed resource in ministry so that these clergy may have a ministry which fulfills their vocation, and so that our beleaguered urban missions will have extra hands to help them. We are only in the early stages of working this ministry through and understanding the results it may have upon our mode of operation. It sounds exciting and romantic to have, let's say, three or four part-time nonstipendiaries occupying a rectory in the inner city; but if they are working all day, who is there to answer the hospital calls? Who is there to coordinate their work? Will they stay over a period of time? Do they have tenure? What is the role of the vestry in relationship to such a community? Will they tend to be too romantic and unrealistic for the seasoned pragmatism of their people? We must try.

Another hopeful sign is the way by which many of our inner-city churches are planning together—sharing budgets, sharing missionary strategy, sharing clergy, sharing ideas. The only danger here is their own solidarity. They can become special-interest groups within the life of the diocese and can tend to be divisive.

The very hopelessness of many urban leaders makes them welcome, once more, the moral preaching of the Church. I believe we have been timid too long. I believe we should attempt to sift through the financial and political symptoms of our decline and find the moral decisions which lie behind them. Even if we are considered wrong, I think we should lift up the neglect of the old, the poor, the young, the black, and the Spanish-speaking as symptoms of a deep moral irresponsibility within our society. The few times I have attempted to speak forth in recent months the response has been overwhelmingly positive. This may indicate a new way by which we can exercise the so-called prophetic ministry in our cities.

A new pietism has risen among us—the so-called charismatic movement and the new interest in prayer groups, spiritual healing, and the like. These are not all part of the charismatic movement; they have their own particular styles. For instance, once a week in the Cathedral of St. John the Divine a prayer group of between three and four hundred young people sit at the feet of an Anglican woman who seems to be able to reach their spirits as they seek to find the mystery of being. Confessions are growing in some of our old Anglo-Catholic parishes after several years of neglect. With great enthusiasm, the clergy attend classes in spiritual direction. In some cases, of course, this is an escape; but I believe that in most cases it is the plumbing of the wellspring of the Spirit for strength and guidance in a day when that guidance is not coming from without.

One of the most disturbing elements of this decade is the absence of the strong social energy of the sixties. During those years the Church could respond to "God's work in the world" and rightfully. But now, with the exception of the women's liberation movement and the recent gay liberation movement, it is hard to find such energy. The cities are strangely quiet. The energy of anger is turned inward and the pattern is apathy, anxiety, and fear. Dare we try to touch, even unleash, energies beneath this fear—and if we dare, how do we touch it? This is a question only the spirit will ask or answer, but it is a question that we must keep asking so that when the time comes, and we are given an opening, we'll respond with excitement and leadership.

It is hard to tell the future. The kind of programing the National Church did in the sixties—the General Convention Special Programs (GCSP)—was giving grants to energetic secular groups which were working toward liberation. But now it's harder to find such groups. There are a few of them, but they are less effective. Should our money be going in grants in that direction? Or should we rather be dealing with the issues that overarch particular ethnic characteristics so that they will have an excited concern for their brothers and sisters in the cities from which they themselves earn their living? I find that people today are sick and tired of hearing about poverty, of hearing about the city; they want to turn it off. Yet, they could not live in the beautiful suburbs were it not for the poor who are living in the ghetto. As Christians, we must bring them to see that they are indeed their brothers' keepers.

I hope we will once more develop a network throughout the Church of those who are socially concerned, flexible, taking many forms, but giving us all a sense of comradeship in the struggle. We have been alone too long since the great movements of the sixties; it is time that we shared our ideas and our enthusiasms as well as our hurts and our fears. I hope that out of the next Convention a plan may arise to effect this.

The cities are dying, and we seek their resurrection. I hope those who read this book will seriously analyze what makes for the dying of their own cities, and will see how each in his own way can respond responsibly to turning the trend around and being part of the rising, not the dying.

chapter 19

THE CHURCH AND HUNGER: THE ONGOING CHALLENGE

Norman J. Faramelli

The media coverage given to world hunger in 1974 and 1975 is fading in 1976. Nevertheless, the problems of famine and malnutrition persist, even if some of their acute signs have been arrested. Therefore, it is now time to realize that the problems of world and domestic hunger are neither novel nor temporary. They have been with us for generations, and experts predict they will worsen over the next ten years and beyond.

Domestic and world hunger are really the tip of an ugly iceberg. The root problem is the inequitable distribution of limited resources which are becoming increasingly expensive. Thus, it is only natural that in the United States and abroad those with the least purchasing power—the poor— are the most adversely affected. Although the global hunger crisis has been exacerbated by soaring population, droughts and flooding, its root cause is seen in the widening gap between the rich and the poor nations. In the United States, lopsided income and wealth distribution patterns have worsened because of spiraling inflation and high unemployment rates.

I. ISSUES AND RESPONSES

The temporary lull in media coverage on hunger should in no way be interpreted as a long-term solution to the problem. About thirty-two poor nations are still cited on the United Nation's "most seriously affected" list—nations with serious hunger/malnutrition problems which rely heavily upon outside food assistance. Another eighty nations grow enough food to feed their people, but they export it for foreign exchange, and hence are forced to import food to nourish their own populations. The income per person in many poor nations ranges from $50 to $200 per year; and even that low figure glosses over the inequities that exist within a nation. In the United States about thirty to forty million people are still living under poverty conditions. For example, a family of three (a mother and two children) in Waltham, Massachusetts, lives on $282 a month, the amount allotted by the welfare department in one of the more "generous" states. Such examples, unfortunately, are not unusual in the United States.

Most food experts claim that beyond 1985 the problems will seriously worsen unless global population is stabilized. Despite agricultural increases, food production has not kept pace with the population explosion. This observation has led many to formulate the wrong conclusion—that overpopulation, not poverty, is the problem. Yet the best evidence of scientists and researchers indicates a close correlation between eradicating poverty and stabilizing population in a humane manner. In sections of India, for instance, population control became effective only after the basic social and economic conditions were improved.

The responses to the world hunger crisis are varied in the Churches—those who feel that if people are hungry, we have a moral obligation to feed them; others who believe that global economic and social development is the only answer; and even some who think the task is utterly hopeless unless population is stabilized. It is encouraging, however, that many are beginning to appreciate the long-term nature of the problems and to realize that the simplistic notion of giving food to hungry people is not necessarily the most appropriate response. Some say it is necessary to teach people to grow wheat instead of sending them wheat. Of course, that demands agricultural tools and arable land. But even after a farmer grows wheat it is imperative that the social and economic conditions be such that the wheat grown is not confiscated by the affluent in or out of the country. Hence, solutions to world hunger should range from food aid to enabling people to become self-reliant in food production. But that cannot happen without fundamental political, social, and economic changes.

Therefore, the ingredients of a solution should include:

—— Food aid for emergency situations, including the establishment of an internationally controlled grain reserve.
——Improved research and development so that tropical countries can improve farming methods to increase their agricultural production.
——Basic changes in political, social, and economic conditions to allow conception control methods to be effective.

In the domestic arena we will need:

—Decent human services for all in need, including the *right* to adequate food, clothing, shelter, and medical care, or a guaranteed adequate income for all.

—The creation of jobs in the public and private sectors so that United States society can approach full employment.

Unfortunately, space does not permit us to give each of these the scrutiny and detail it deserves. Nevertheless, these are among the issues that people serious about global and domestic poverty—and the resulting hunger problem—will have to address.

II. THE CHURCH CONFRONTS WORLD DOMESTIC HUNGER

Our task is not to offer a detailed analysis of the issues but to explore the crucial role that the Church can play. One of the most difficult problems encountered will be helping Church people move beyond the immediate, emotional response of "send food to the hungry" to the root causes of world/domestic hunger. Part of our religious conditioning has been to respond immediately in charity and compassion to those in real need. Although such instincts are valuable, they lead to inadequate analyses and only partial solutions. For instance, much more than emergency food aid is needed to cope creatively with hunger.

The revised guidelines of the Presiding Bishop's Fund For World Relief show movement beyond relief and rehabilitation to development projects and basic development education, and should be widely encouraged and supported. Love, in its broadest Christian sense, is rooted in social justice, not charity. And that is reflected in the fund's guidelines. Love should lead people to a new self-realization and self-reliance, and not foster dependent relationships. That can be said even if we realize that aid is often necessary in emergency situations. Nevertheless, we should note the twin problems of sustained aid—it places the recipient in a dependency relationship to the donor, and gives the donor enormous political clout over the recipient. Neither is desirable.

Another difficult problem in facing the hunger dilemma is to help people see that the issue cannot be relegated to a long list of extraneous social action projects, but is integral to our understanding of the Christian faith. Traditionally, social justice issues such as hunger have been treated as peripheral to the ongoing life of the Church. They were usually funded out of our surplus funds and were viewed as an "extra" or "nice thing" as long as the Church could afford them. That surplus is fast diminishing, and in the future the Church will confront one of two options: a) either it will abandon issues such as hunger or b) it will reinterpret them convincingly as being integral to our understanding of the Gospel.

Currently, the movement away from the funding of Church and society programs is not only due to a backlash against the social activism of the 60s, but is a reflection of the financial crunch affecting the entire Church. If hunger is treated as just one peripheral social concern, the Church will surely bypass it, save for token efforts at relief aid and Thanksgiving baskets.

There is a necessity to link personal spiritual development with social issues such as hunger. There are religious and theological as well as moral reasons for our involvement in hunger issues. It is not satisfactory to sound moral appeals of "you ought" and "you must," but we need to declare the saving love that God has, is, and will show to all humanity through Jesus Christ. Because of that love we are asked to respond, not just out of a sense of moral duty or obligation, but as an indication of our gracious thanksgiving. Most of us tire easily when subjected to moral tirades, even when we think they are justified.

The Gospel tells us repeatedly that the love of God and the love of others are inseparable (I John 3-4, Matt. 25:31ff), that the love of God is expressed in our caring for others. Our biblical heritage tells us that we find spiritual fulfillment in life only when we devote ourselves to God's service. That is, meaning and purpose are not found in self-aggrandizement but in service to others. "For whoever would save his life will lose it, and whoever loses his life for my sake and the gospel's will save it" (Mark 8:35).

As the Church faces the hunger issue, it has to end once and for all those senseless debates about whether personal piety or social change is the authentic expression of the Gospel. It is not a case of "spirituality *vs.* political action," as the modern world would like to polarize it. There is no social Gospel; there is no personal Gospel. There is only one Gospel of Jesus Christ which has both social and personal dimensions. To emphasize one at the expense of the other is to distort and ultimately to betray the Gospel message.

Therefore, we are called to engage in hunger issues not only because of a sense of moral duty, but as a gracious response to God's loving concern for us, and with the understanding that it is through such participation that we experience our own spiritual development.

III. FOUR TASKS FOR THE CHURCH

As the Church approaches the hunger issue it has to engage, in an ongoing way, four crucially related tasks. These are not necessarily to be dealt with sequentially, but each should be a vital component in our response, and in the response we help others to make.

(1) Spiritual Nourishment. The issues of world/domestic hunger are enormous in scope, technical in nature, and tend to scare off the non-experts. When we come to grips with the complexity of the solutions, there is a tendency to become overwhelmed, perplexed, and even paralyzed. Hence, a necessary starting point is for one to be not only in the proper frame of mind, but to receive the necessary spiritual nourishment to be in the proper state of soul. We should explore, understand, and internalize the theological roots of our involvement.

Discovering our theological roots goes far beyond providing a biblical basis with appropriate proof-texts on hunger and social justice. We should understand the entire heritage with its insights, promises, and judgments revealed through our biblical and Church traditions. Our tradition teaches us, contrary to the conventional wisdom, that God champions the cause of the poor, the disenfranchised, and the dispossessed. Although God loves all, the biblical deity is peculiarly lopsided in favor of the outcasts—those without power and influence (Jer.22; Is.1:17;58). The liberation of Israelite slaves from Egyptian oppression stands as a central biblical motif (Ex.3).

In the coming of Christ, God has shattered the conventional wisdom (I Cor.1:20–25). That belief not only provides us with new modes of discernment, it empowers us to do that which we are called to do. In issues of long duration, such as world/domestic hunger, it is inadequate simply to become involved; we need the sustaining power of God's presence to help us keep the commitments we made. In light of the long-term nature of the issues, sustained spiritual enrichment is an absolute necessity. When the battle seems uphill, the sense of purpose grows nebulous, the objectives appear unattainable, and it is easy to lose faith and quit. At such times we will truly understand and appreciate the value of the spiritual nourishment we obtain through private prayer and meditation, Bible study, and corporate worship, especially the Eucharist. Our corporate worship can also provide us with the necessary support group in whom we can confide and to whom we can be accountable. The Gospel provides the necessary "staying power" to deal with hunger.

(2) Motivation. As we respond and get others to respond to hunger issues, we should explore the motivational factors. That is: What really motivates us? The Gospel calls us to new life and possibility, yet often hunger appeals have been oriented toward guilt feelings that produce spontaneous acts of compassion. That is one of the problems of viewing photographs depicting the distended stomachs of malnourished children. They evoke images of guilt and pity rather than social justice.

Appeals to guilt, whether direct or indirect, are often counterproductive. The response they produce is shortlived, and often the guilt-ridden person is either soon turned off or is psychologically paralyzed into inaction or misguided action.

The Gospel message says little about long-term guilt, other than that Christ has conquered the powers of sin and death, and that we should act accordingly. Any guilt feeling should be only the prelude to repentance, and repentance leads to forgiveness, justification, redemption, and a life of new hope and possibility. Jesus did not call people to feel guilty about their life-styles but to change them (Luke 12:15). Hence, the promises of God and the opportunity for new life should be our primary motivating force as we call people to participate in the struggles of the hungry.

(3)Education. Our education on the hunger issue does not mean simply the exposure to copious facts and details about the food crisis. Authentic education has to deal with the relationships of institutions—political and economic—and their involvement in the root causes of hunger. For example: How do United States trade and aid programs affect development patterns in poor nations? What is the role of transnational corporations in perpetuating or solving global poverty? What is the link between a new United States weapon system and our capacity to deal with domestic poverty? These are difficult questions indeed, but ones that must be answered. It is difficult, yet vitally important, to achieve the proper balance. On the one hand, one needs enough information and analysis to make intelligent decisions. But on the other, one needs to avoid the "information overload" syndrome that easily confuses one into inaction.

Another educational task is to form and sharpen our critical faculties to deal with the tough ethical choices. When we deal with large scale issues, by what criteria do we decide what is the proper moral posture? Our religious heritage should enable us to develop critical ethical sensitivities based on our understanding of social justice and stewardship—that is, we should be able to make the "best" decision when the options are complex; and the "right" decision cannot be perceived in simple right or wrong categories.

(4)Action Steps. Along with spiritual nourishment, proper motivation, and sound education (in analyzing the issues and making ethical decisions), action steps have to be undertaken. In fact, these four components make sense only when they are worked on together.

There is a tendency in the Church to seek personal solutions to the hunger problems, not only because of the Church's individualistic bias but because personal action steps seem possible, while the social, political, and economic factors seem inaccessible or remote. Yet despite the temptations, we all have to be reminded that there are no personal solutions to structural or systemic questions. For example, the grain that we save by not eating meat will not automatically find its way to hungry stomachs. That will occur only if the appropriate political and economic decisions are made. Fasting has enormous symbolic value, and by no means should be debased, but fasting should serve as a reminder of what has to be done in the political and economic arenas, which are the twin centers of major decision-making in society. No personal life-style change in consumption, even if profound, will influence or alter institutional realities.

Of course, both social and personal action steps are needed. Although it might be naïve to think that there are personal solutions to social problems, it is hypocritical to speak of systemic changes unless we are willing to deal with and accept the consequences of such changes in our lives and in the lives of others. If we are serious about feeding hungry people, however, we cannot sidestep the political and economic aspects, even when the Church's involvement in these generates controversies.

We should not expect the entire Church to take a leadership role in political action programs. Many honest and dedicated Church people do not have that inclination, but can find meaningful engagement in other ways. Thus, the Church program has to be as varied as its constituents. Some parishioners will enter the issue through Bible study and liturgy, others through sacrifice and fasting, and still others will focus on specific domestic and international hunger projects. Church people can enter the hunger arena through the phase at which they seem most comfortable and capable. Nevertheless, the necessity of economic and political changes should never be short-circuited. Historically, these are the aspects of the hunger issue that the Church finds easiest to ignore. That is why special emphasis has to be given to food policy issues, and support given to ecumenical groups working on them.

CONCLUSION

The hunger challenge facing the world and the Church is one of long-term duration. Hence, we need to discard that "crisis" or short-term mentality that conveys the wrong images. We need to put on the "whole armour of God" and gear up for the long haul (Eph.6).

As Christians we proceed, not in the naïve assumption that the problems have easy solutions but in the hope that history is in the hands of a living, righteous, and loving God. That affirmation gives us assurance that God not only expects us to make commitments to feed the hungry, but will empower us to honor the commitments we make, especially during those moments when the possibility of genuine solutions seems faint.

The Church and Hunger: The Ongoing Challenge 157

We also preceed with the understanding that our spiritual development, and even our personal salvation, is linked with our involvement in such issues as hunger. Lastly, it is through showing our concern for the "least of the brethren," and by participating in their struggles, that we find meaning and purpose to life and ultimately experience spiritual fulfillment.

chapter 20

MEDICINE: SOME QUESTIONS ABOUT ITS FUTURE

Clifton K. Meador, M.D.

In responding to the request to give my opinion about the future of medicine, I have elected to examine a particular but representative group of people who now come to doctors. These are people who have complaints but in whom no medical disease can be found. There are no precise figures, but estimates indicate that this group comprise somewhere between sixty and seventy-five percent of all people who come to physicians. Whatever this figure may be, most observers agree these people pose a major problem for the present and the future. It is my opinion that the nature of the future of medicine will hinge on how it will deal with this large group.

In this paper I will examine some of the historical origins of this problem. Since the present management of these people is often unsatisfactory and confusing for both physician and patient, I will take a close look at what might be called a contract that now exists between a physician and a patient. I will attempt to do this by taking the long-standing, unspoken understanding between physician and patient and making it an open, explicit contract. It is my contention that the nature of this existing contract and the beliefs that go with it are part of the cause of this problem.

Since the diagnostic process is central to understanding any encounter between physician and patient, I will describe it in some detail, pointing out both its strengths and limitations, particularly as it relates to people who have symptoms but no demonstrable medical disease. Finally, I will speculate about what I believe to be the nature of some of these people and raise some questions about the future of medicine as it relates to them.

SOME HISTORICAL ORIGINS OF THE PROBLEM

Dr. Sidney Garfield of the Kaiser Foundation has looked at the changing mix of people who come to see physicians. Before the turn of the century, it was mostly seriously sick people with life-threatening diseases who came to see a physician. They could expect very little. They either died or recovered. Physicians had little more than compassion to offer. Slowly, as medicine made scientific advances, patients came with earlier and earlier symptoms of disease. Garfield calls these the "early sick." By the 1920s and 1930s, the population coming to see physicians included both the "sick and early sick."

Following World War II, scientific medicine made many advances. Most notably the antibiotics appeared and many infectious diseases became curable rather than lethal. These and other scientific successes were widely publicized. Slowly, other people started to turn to medicine. By the middle 1950s, the "well" and "worried well" were added to the mix of people coming to see the physician. Instead of seeing only the "sick and early sick," after 1950 the physician was confronted with a steadily increasing number of "well and worried well" people. The well wanted to stay well and the worried well wanted the widely popularized miracles they read about. Thus a system trained and tooled for diagnoisis and care of sick people was now flooded with well people or people with worries who looked to medicine for a cure. Medicine's important successes became a source of its problems. Although Garfield's writings have been much publicized, some physicians still tend to operate as though only sick people were coming to them. There is still not a universal awareness that the mix of people has radically changed. This subtle and largely unnoticed change in the mix of people coming to the doctor is a large part of the problem I wish to discuss.

THE NATURE OF THE CONTRACT BETWEEN PHYSICIAN AND PATIENT

Behind any unwritten contract is a set of beliefs that remain largely subconscious. Out of these subconscious beliefs will come expectations that are an unwritten part of any contract. These subconscious beliefs are what I hope to set out in explicit terms. I assume that most physicians want and intend to do their best to help their patients. I also assume that most patients want to be well and healthy. I assign no conscious or malicious intent in any of the following. They are simply my descriptions of unconscious beliefs and the implicit contract as I believe them to be held by many physicians and patients.

THE CONTRACT AS VIEWED BY THE PATIENT

Many of the patients I see for the first time, whether or not they turn out to have a demonstrable medical disease, seem to be thinking something like this: "I am in pain or anguish. The trouble seems to be only in my body. If it is not relieved I will get sicker or die. You are a physician but you are also a kind of magician. You will always be able to find out very specifically what is wrong with me and give it a name. You will either give me a pill for it or you may have to recommend an operation to remove the sick part of me. Either way you alone will remove my pain and anguish. The only thing I have to do is follow your instructions. I had nothing whatever to do with this illness. It just came out of the blue like some evil force. In no way is my mind playing any role in my disease."

There are many variations on this basic theme and many complex and symbolic components. Whatever they may be, the fundamental belief is that the physician will be a scientific magician. The patient has read about the miracles of penicillin, cortisone, hormones, even heart transplants. He has come to see medicine as perfect, and imperfections as malpractice. He disowns any responsibility for his own illness and sees himself in purely a passive role with the physician.

THE CONTRACT AS VIEWED BY THE PHYSICIAN

The physician too has his own beliefs about illness. While there are also many differences in these, I have chosen what I believe to be a common view of many modern physicains. It happens to be the belief I held until a few years ago. The beliefs and contract of the physician might go something like this: "My job is to find the patient's disease, give it a name and, if possible, treat it. Medicine has made great advances and we are nearing perfection in our diagoistic methods. Of course, there are many diseases for which there is no effective treatment, but in most cases I can find the disease and make a diagnosis. If there is a treatment, I give the appropriate medicine or recommend an operation.

"Disease is usually caused by a single foreign agent (virus, fungus, bacteria) or by a single biochemical abnormality within the body. In most cases there is only a single cause.

"Although I have not given it much thought, I believe the mind and body are separated. Diseases either arise in the body (organic disease) or in the mind (functional or psychiatric disease). When a patient has symptoms in his body and I cannot find a disease in his body, then he either has a psychiatric disease or he is imagining his symptoms. Most of the time I can find some disease in the body which will explain the patient's symptoms."

The statements of the patient and the physician are obviously very similar. There is an overtone of the magical in the patient which is missing in the physician. Otherwise, the two beliefs are almost identical. Both believe strongly in the near perfection of the diagnostic method. Both see the physician in the active role and the patient in the passive one. There is no disagreement on the nature of the disease although the patient tends to see it as more evil. The physician sees it as bad luck. Finally, both patient and physician see mind and body as separated. It is the almost complete agreement in belief that makes any fallacies and weaknesses virtually invisible to either party. Both parties seem committed to finding a disease in the body, naming it, and proceeding with medical or surgical treatment.

By these views, the body is seen as a kind of machine and the physician as a mechanic. In the intensive care unit with a severely ill patient, the beliefs are almost valid. The physician, almost independently, must assume an active role and move rapidly to make decisions and proceed with diagnosis and therapy. There is little quarrel with the contract in that setting. But that is not where most encounters occur. Most people come into contact with medicine long before the situation is critical and they do it on an outpatient basis. It is this vast majority of ambulatory patients that I will be discussing throughout this paper, particularly those patients who have symptoms but no demonstrable medical disease.

THE DIAGNOSTIC PROCESS

The physician operates with three basic bits of data to arrive at a diagnosis. The patient describes his complaints, or *symptoms* (pains, shortness of breath, fatigue, bleeding from some orifice, and so on). The physician then looks for *signs* on the physical examination (murmurs in the heart, masses on palpation). A sign is anything the physician can see, feel, hear, smell, or, in the old days, taste in a patient. From symptoms and signs, the physician will think of several disease possibilities and order the appropriate laboratory or X-ray test to confirm or refute his postulate.

It is a kind of triangulation process similar to three-point navigation. Assume that all of medical disease is a circle and that signs, symptoms, and laboratory tests are looking out across all diseases from three points on the circle's edge. The symptoms cut a wedge across the circle, signs cut another wedge, and laboratory tests cut a third. The common area, or area of intersection, of all three represents a single diagnosis or several diagnoses. If the symptoms are vague and general, a very large wedge will be cut. For example, weakness or fatigue are very general symptoms and therefore suggest an endless number of diseases. Pain after eating is much more specific and suggests a relatively short list of diseases and, in my analogy, a very small wedge across the circle of all diseases.

From the list of diseases suggested by the symptoms and signs, special laboratory or X-ray tests can be used to narrow the possibilities. The process is repeated until only a single disease (or several diseases in some cases) can be documented. A diagnosis is then said to be made.

It should be obvious that in the absence of signs or symptoms, a physician is almost at a loss to know where to begin. Although not obvious, it is true that symptoms, more than signs, account for directing the physician. There are many diseases with symptoms but no signs (angina pectoris, migraine headache, duodenal ulcer, some tuberculosis, cancers of all sorts, and on and on). There are very few diseases where signs can exist for any period before symptoms occur. This severe limitation of the physical examination is not widely appreciated. Thus, it is symptoms that direct the physician in his logical step-by-step diagnostic process. Of course, there are a few patients with very early disease who have no symptoms but this is a very short-lived stage. In general, if a patient has absolutely no symptoms, he can assume himself to be in good health.

As an example of the success of the diagnostic process and its appropriate application, say a patient gives symptoms of weakness, faintness on standing, weight loss, and an increasing pigmentation of the skin. He also has noticed a craving for salty foods. The astute physician will think of only a few possibilities with this list of symptoms. He might think of widespread cancer, salt-losing kidney disease, or adrenal insufficiency (lack of cortisone).

From the physical examination, he confirms the deep tanning of the skin and also notices loss of axillary hair. He finds the blood pressure to be on the low side and to fall when the patient stands. From these symptoms and signs he narrows his list of what to look for, either kidney disease or adrenal insufficiency. Renal disease is excluded by the appropriate blood tests. The physician then measures the level of cortisone in the blood. The levels are very low and cannot be stimulated to rise, thus confirming the diagnosis of adrenal gland insufficiency due to destruction of the adrenal glands (so-called Addison's disease). He gives the patient cortisone tablets and all of the symptoms disappear. The patient returns from a moribund state and regains his weight and strength. The blood pressure returns to normal. The patient is now completely well and will remain so as long as he takes his daily cortisone tablets to replace his missing hormone.

This is a very powerful and exciting experience for both physician and patient. I have chosen Addison's disease as my example for several reasons. It is almost the prototype for what both physician and patient believe about disease. A single defect is found and replaced, and complete recovery follows. It is what all physicians and patients hope for with every encounter. It is the kind of experience that more and more patients have come to expect. Addison's disease is a very rare disease, however, and there are very few diseases so clearly definable and treatable. Yet it is almost a model of the power of modern scientific medicine at its best. It is the existence of this kind of single defect that is easily treated that has led the public to come to medicine in large numbers. Unfortunately, their expectations are unrealistically high.

FAILURES AND LIMITATIONS OF THE DIAGNOSTIC PROCESS

The diagnostic process as I have described it has its greatest power in finding medical disease in a symptomatically critically sick patient. It runs into great difficulties in patients with symptoms yet no demonstrable medical disease.

Take, for example, the common patient who complains of several general symptoms: headaches, slight nausea, fatigue, and occasional dizziness. The physical examination is entirely within normal limits. There are no signs of disease. At first the general laboratory and X-ray studies are within normal limits. Even later, with more exhaustive studies, the results remain within normal limits. It is at this point that trouble begins and the common beliefs of both physician and patient come into a kind of conflict. Curiously, the conflict comes from their apparent similarity of beliefs, not from their differences, and neither party clearly sees the conflict.

For the physician, he has applied his method to the fullest and has found no disease. His beliefs and model have been confronted; and all too often he jumps prematurely from having found no disease to a conclusion that there is no disease. Since the patient's disease cannot be found, it is inferred that it does not exist. Therefore, the patient is thought to be imagining his symptoms. Holding to his belief in the separation of mind and body, he may tell the patient (although from no direct observation) that it must be "just nerves." For whatever reason, the physician is at this uncertain point: his powerful model has run out. From all his training and experience (most of it with critically ill patients) he knows the model and his beliefs are valid. The model can find pneumonia, meningitis, acute appendicitis, Addison's disease, even tumors in the remotest part of the brain. It can identify many single hormone deficiencies and anemias of all sorts. He has seen it work time and time again. But here he has applied it, even exhausted it, and before him sits a patient with symptoms yet no disease. Both his model and his beliefs cannot be wrong about this patient.

He sees the patient as unreasonable and complaining. The physician often projects his own discomfort with uncertainty onto the patient. He may even tell his colleagues he examined another "crock."

The patient's reaction to this is understandably confused. He believes as strongly as the physician in the diagnostic medical model and in the powers of scientific medicine. He also believes strongly in the separation of mind and body. The slightest inference that the disease is not present in the body infers disease of the mind, and he will be seen as imagining his symptoms. He understandably resists all efforts of the physician to tell him that his disease is in his mind. He hurts or suffers in his body; therefore his body is sick. He does not feel nervous, so how can it be "just nerves"?

This insistence by the patient and his rigid belief in the medical model subtly drives the physician into other ways of dealing with this kind of patient. He can continue to press on with many laboratory and X-ray studies (no longer clearly directed by symptoms or signs) until he finds an abnormality (*any* abnormality, no matter how inconsequential), even a variation of normal, or worse, a false positive laboratory test. In almost all cases, the alleged abnormality will have little or nothing to do with the patient's symptoms. It is simply a false diagnosis. In many cases, neither the physician nor the patient is aware that this has happened. A label has been found. The "trouble" has been discovered and named. This discovery relieves the physician. He is no longer confronted by uncertainty. His powerful model is satisfied and still powerful. He does not have to confront a patient full of bodily symptoms with the fuzzy and always unsatisfactory explanation that he can find "nothing wrong."

As for the patient, he avoids the stigma and fright of being told that "it's just your nerves," and the awful inference that he is imagining his symptoms. He has a name for his troubles and he has a legitimate, albeit false, disease. His belief in medicine is reconfirmed. Both physician and patient are pleased, at least for the short run. Neither is even slightly aware of the illusion which surrounds them.

Whatever may have been the true source of the patient's problems in the first place is now buried forever in a false label. If the origins of the symptoms were indeed psychological, then the patient will continue with his life-long symptoms, always referring them to his falsely labeled disease. He will enter an incurable stage and remain there for life, never facing or dealing with the real causes of his problems and symptoms. In terms of our current problems of an overloaded medical system, these patients return again and again, using inordinate amounts of time and resources with no real hope of personal growth or recovery so long as they hold on to their false disease. Since patients with symptoms but with no

Medicine: Some Questions about its Future

truly demonstrable medical disease are very common, they constitute a group of major users of physicians' time.

It should be clear that considerable harm can come to these patients and that it can come from several sources. Both the public and the physician often have an unrealistic belief in the powers of the diagnostic process. Medicine has not yet been able to face its uncertainty. Surely, there must be very large areas of knowledge about disease and about man that are not yet discovered. Neither the public nor the physician seem ready to accept this, and out of this unwillingness come all sorts of vague and falsely labeled diseases. Certainty about a label, even though false, seems to be preferred to uncertainty even when it is closer to the truth.

In my opinion, the major source of harm comes from our deep belief that man can be divided into a mind and a body. It is not within my power or experience to build a firm and convincing argument against this belief. It is my experience, however, that this embedded belief and our fears of anything "mental" are at the core of the problem I am discussing, both for physicians and patients. It seems we will go to all ends to avoid any implication that our mind or our thoughts are in any way a source of our symptoms. The leap in belief that is required in order to see that processes within the mind can effect bodily function seems to be beyond the grasp of many people. Part of our resistance must also come from our new and still limited ability to deal with these kinds of problems effectively. For example, it is easier to give penicillin for pneumonia than it is to listen for and deal with tensions and conflicts which might be causing gastric contractions.

What is going on in these people who run to physicians with symptoms yet no demonstrable disease? I have seen no reported comprehensive study characterizing all of these patients. I can only draw from my own experience and make a few statements about some of them. First, although Garfield's concept of the "worried well" has some utility, I would reject it as a general category for all of these patients. The group is probably so heterogeneous that it will defy any neat classification.

Some of these patients probably do have a medical disease which is either beyond existing knowledge or beyond the limits of our methods. Some are ingesting, breathing, or coming into contact with some agent which may be uniquely noxious only to that person. I heard of a recent patient who found that her toothpaste was causing diarrhea and abdominal pain. Others have learned, at a deep and unconscious level, that symptoms produce sympathy and attention. They are better off with symptoms than they were before they had them. (There is a secondary gain to all illness.) Still others are caught up in tensions and conflicts in their lives and from these develop a variety of body symptoms. There seems to be a small group who are trapped unconsciously in some bizarre game of win-lose with the physician. In many patients there are heavy and rigid religious views which seem to be beyond even biologic capability, so that these people live in perpetual conflict between their human needs and their religious beliefs; and there are many other subgroups too numerous to list.

Since these people with symptoms but with no documentable medical disease constitute a majority of patients seeing physicians, it is my opinion that the manner in which medicine moves to deal with these problems will largely determine its future. Of equal or greater importance will be the public's acceptance or rejection of medicine's future moves. At present it appears to me that many of these people are medicalized into patients with false diagnoses for all of the reasons I have stated.

The unraveling of these problems now and in the future will not be simple, and I can only approach it by a series of questions.

Will medicine continue to focus almost exclusively on diseases that can only be defined in biomolecular or anatomic abnormalities, excluding all others as imaginary or beyond the profession?

OR

Will medicine reject the mind-body dichotomy and see man as an indivisible organism, subject to all manner of stimuli and their ill effects, whether or not they can yet be described in biomolecular terms?

Will medicine continue to believe that diseases arising in the body take some higher priority and are therefore more real than disorders of thought and feelings?

OR

Will medicine learn to see that human pain and anguish are all equal for consideration no matter what form they may take?

Will the public continue to rush to medicine, unrealistically seeking miraculous cures for problems that come from within?

OR

Will the public gain deeper awareness of their own selves and learn to deal with their own problems more directly and honestly through other helping people and institutions?

Will the public and medicine see that present medical science is far from perfect and will remain so for a long, long time, if not always?

Will we learn to see pain and anguish as sometimes positive messages for change or will we continue to see them only as feelings to fear and avoid and be removed by pills or surgery?

Can we ever learn to live comfortably with life as an uncertain thing and death as inevitable? Can we do this without creating illusions that are daily shattered by each new scientific discovery or without taking massive amounts of Valium to numb us?

In the overall scheme of things, the medical profession is a very small bit. At present it looms almost as some major force, holding out and being held out as more than it can deliver. When will medicine and the public define its proper place so that it neither denies its more general helping role nor draws to it all of human misery in the guise of medical disease?

COMMENTARY BY THE REV. BENJAMIN B. SMITH

Dr. Meador's article is a challenge to the Church to take seriously its own basic beliefs. Man is a whole, and cannot be reduced to a body-mind dichotomy—no more than truth can be dichotomized between scientific and theological, or medical and religious. In the search for truth, the future of medicine is coterminus with the future of the Church, for the most promising sign of the future is the diminishing, if not the elimination, of false dichotomies, leaving us open to learn.

The Church has shared in the development of the present state of medicine, with its participation in illusion, its promise of magical power, and its separation of mind and body. The Church participates by abandoning its traditional concern for the whole man—including the human body, its health and disease—to the physicians and their scientific and technological processes. We have expected them to provide the answers to the problems which have their source in the deep recesses of the human condition.

Soul-searching by physicians alone will not be adequate in seeking a broader definition of the contract between patients and physicians. The Church can play a more active role in "demythologizing" the excessive claims implicit in the dramatic advances of scientific medicine. Inasmuch as basic beliefs regarding magical powers, defects and diseases, human potentialities and limitations, the nature and structure of man, and the phenomenon of death are involved, the Church can provide the theological concepts which lead to a more realistic, and therefore intrinsically more healthy, perspective on human life.

The parish church offers a potential screening clinic, where clergy and trained lay people, in close liaison with physicians and other medical professionals, can provide a multifaceted approach to the human problems that often express themselves in symptoms. The parish church can develop programs geared to the reduction and management of stress, the development of health-inducing life-styles, the development of human support systems. It can, with the assistance of physicians and other health professionals, offer self-help programs with an emphasis upon a realistic assessment of symptoms, basic management of the problems accessible to self-management, the distinction between symptoms that require a physician's attention and those that do not, and, primarily, an emphasis upon a realistic assessment of what and what not to expect from the physician's attention.

The parish church can be restored to its once-accepted role of provider of primary health care. What is needed in order to regain this position is a reassessment of the nature of health; a restoration of the responsibility of the individual for the maintenance of his own health; a sense of what it means, in terms of self-acceptance as a whole being, to be "well"—a dynamic personal organism of enormous complexity interacting with its social, emotional, and physical environment with a series of consequences which manifest themselves, on occasion, as symptoms.

The questions raised by the present situation are theological as well as medical. If there is to be a reassesment, it will come through mutual soul-searching involving religion and medicine.

chapter 21

CURRENT ETHICAL ISSUES: AN OVERVIEW

James M. Childress

A recent Gallup poll (see *The Washington Post*, April 18, 1976) indicates that sixty-six percent of those interviewed believe that morality is declining. They believe that people are less honest and moral than they used to be. In 1965, fifty-two percent held a similar view, while in 1952 only forty-six percent thought that morality was declining. Despite the notorious limitations of opinion polls, this widespread sense of a moral decline is worth noting. It is not necessary to hold that morality depends on religion in order to be interested in the moral implications of religion or in the way religion contributes to the moral ethos. Moralty is logically independent of religion, and there is no good evidence that religion is essential as a psychological or sociological support for moral conduct. Although religion is not necessary for morality, it may contribute significantly to moral decisions and conduct.

What is the Church's responsibility for social morality or public ethics? First of all, the Church is to be itself, to be true to itself. This is perhaps its most significant social ethic. But in addition, one of its functions is to be what James Gustafson calls "a community of moral discourse," to explore the ethical implications of theological affirmations and loyalties, and to test the meaning and application of ethical norms. If the Church exercises this function only in dramatic crises, it fails in its responsibility, for it needs to identify and illuminate moral issues in ordinary, day-to-day decisions.

One should not suppose that the articulation of general principles and values will suffice. Church people, among others, often participate in a consensus about general principles and values (nondiscrimination between members of different races, for example) and yet fail to connect these standards to concrete decisions and actions. (See, for instance, Jeffrey Hadden, *The Gathering Storm in the Churches.* New York: Doubleday, 1966.) Case studies as part of the moral discourse—whether educational or actual—are invaluable, for they help to fill in what could easily remain empty and vacuous. Even case studies, of course, do not guarantee a transition from general or particular judgments to decision and action, as critics of Lawrence Kohlberg's theory of moral development have emphasized.

It is tempting to oversimplify decision-making by concentrating on a process of practical reasoning that neglects the imagination. Imagination, in the words of David Erdman, is "reasoning in metaphors." As Stanley Hauerwas, among others, has reminded us, our visions, images, metaphors, and stories shape the way we understand and use principles in concrete situations. One of the Church's main tasks is to develop sensitivity to the metaphorical language that pervades our moral discourse. Some metaphors mislead, others illuminate. For instance, our discussion of scarce resources on a worldwide scale and our proposed solutions hinge on images, metaphors, and analogies. Among the most widely used are Garett Hardin's image of "lifeboat ethics"—moral and legal decisions made in tightly drawn emergencies; and the image of "triage"—the medical practice, especially in emergencies, of sorting victims into priority groups for treatment. Such images may prevent us from seeing what is really at stake; they may mask moral realities. For instance, Stuart Hinds insists that we should not extend the term triage by analogy from a medical to a social context, for it "may permit us to become insulated from the horrors of famine, to abandon the search for alternatives, more humane solutions to the problem, and instead comfortably to commit acts that otherwise would seem monstrous and unjust."

Formally, then, the Church as a community of moral discourse should attend to moral reasoning, including principles and rules, images and metaphors, and theological affirmations in general and in relation to specific cases. If we try to specify the moral issues that the Church will have to face within this framework, our task becomes more perilous. Nevertheless, we can expect considerable success in identifying the *types* of issues that the Church will have to face in the next decade. For instance, the Christian community from its earliest days has had to deal with questions about conscience and the political order, the legitimacy of taking life, and the extent of our positive obligations to our neighbors. We should not allow the latest journalistic fad-mongering to blind us to the persistence of important *types* of ethical questions, even in the apparently novel problems that we face. Rarely, if ever, will we confront a situation that is unparalleled in the history of human reflection or that cannot be illuminated by principles, images, and other concepts that we affirm. Indeed, we would not even recognize a moral problem or dilemma without the use of such moral principles and images. Even in the complex biomedical area, we will have to proceed by exploring the meaning and implications of principles and images. In the wake of certain changes in society or technology, we may well resolve conflicts differently, or weigh principles differently, but such alterations are not identical with *discovering* principles. Most often our moral discourse is analogical as we analyze and compare cases in the light of such principles and images.

VIOLENCE AND WAR

One set of issues that will remain of critical importance in the next decade concerns the use of violence against political orders and war between nations. It is, of course, difficult to generate and sustain attention to issues that do not appear to be immediately relevant or to require immediate decisions. Why, one might ask, should the Church devote attention to the issue of war when the only current wars are "cold" ones? Although questions about whether and when wars can be justified crop up again and again, the Church seems surprised when it has to face another war. Without serious and sustained attention to the moral values, principles, and rules undergirding Christian reflection on war and violence, it is too much to expect consciences to be informed for decisions about future conflicts. Furthermore, to push these questions aside is to fail to see how they pervade numerous activities—the continuing arms race, for example.

The demand not to harm, injure, or kill one's neighbors appears to be a *prima facie* obligation, and it is also an implication of Christian *agape*. Because we tend to whitewash violent means when they appear in the service of ends we cherish, and because the state tries to obliterate feelings of reluctance and guilt in order to create a more efficient fighting machine, one major task for the Church is to keep alive this presumption against the use of violence. Both pacifists and nonpacifists can agree on this task. Pacifists, however, insist that this presumption can never be rebutted, while proponents of just wars spell out the conditions for just and/ or justified wars. In Edward Bond's play *Bingo: Scenes of Money and Death,* a character says "only a god or a devil can write in other men's blood and not ask why they split it and what it cost." Acknowledging that wars appear to be inevitable, just-war theorists insist that some of them can be justified if they meet certain standards—legitimate self-defense or protection of the innocent.

As I suggested, even pacifists can admit a stake in the preservation and rigorous application of just-war standards. I have in mind absolute pacifists, not only technological or nuclear pacifists who have concluded that modern wars are unjustified because our weapons wreak such destruction or do not permit discrimination between combatants and noncombatants. Even if pacifists feel that they cannot participate in any wars, their interest in preserving human life and diminishing the number and frequency of wars may well lead them to insist that nations respect the just-war standards, including just cause, right intentions, last resort, proportionality, and just means. War, *per se,* is not "hell," for there are better and worse wars. Since there are degrees of inhumanity, injustice, and brutality in war, we might expect pacifists to emphasize the *jus in bello,* the laws of war or restraints and limits in war. Even pacifists who condemn the "crime of war" may also recognize "war crimes." But the notion of "war crimes" depends on an understanding of moral and legal standards within war—production of noncombatants and prisoners of war, and avoidance of unnecessary suffering.

If I am right that the Church, including its pacifists and proponents of just wars, has a stake in standards of just war and the laws of war, it must articulate those standards and apply them to actual and hypothetical cases even in peace time. Indeed, the tranquility of relative peace may well provide a setting for the formation of conscience apart from the emotional involvements in a particular war such as Vietnam. The Church cannot assume that Vietnam demonstrated that just-war standards are irrelevant, for, after all, many critics of the war appealed to standards—proportionality or just means, for instance. If the Church has some responsibility for the world's moral discourse and action, it may well affirm and try to strengthen just-war standards, which nations often violate but rarely repudiate.

LOVE AND DISTRIBUTIVE JUSTICE

In addition to their claims of non-injury, our neighbors may also make claims for positive actions. They may stand in need of our beneficent and loving responses according to the Good Samaritan ideal. We should never suppose that the charitable deeds of individual Christians and the Church can be subsumed under the heading of justice. The danger in a complex, interdependent, welfare state is that *voluntary* acts of charity may simply seem irrelevant or meaningless. There is always a place for voluntary Christian actions of love. As Emil Brunner suggested, love can certainly be poured into the cracks and crevices of the institutions of justice. It can add personal care to impersonal mechanisms that are, of course, indispensable. And it can also serve as a transcendent norm to indicate that our achievements, however great they are, fall short of the community of love. Self-giving and self-sacrifice remain virtues that ought to be evoked and demanded by the Christian worldview.

Nevertheless, the Church must face extremely difficult questions of the justice of retribution and distribution in the next decade. Space does not permit me to focus on institutions of punishment. Some of the questions of distributive justice already confront us in painful ways, for they tear away our veils of self-deception and expose our own selfishness and complacency. And yet they also indicate that benevolence or charity is not enough. How do we respond to the claims of "future generations" or "statistical lives"—unknown persons in possible future danger—regarding the environment or genetic engineering? Or how do we respond to the claims of persons in other countries faced with famine and starvation? That is, how do we respond effectively, not only in our voluntary associations but also through our government? What is the fitting response that is both right and effective?

Clearly the Church must acknowledge the truth about itself, its members, and the society of which it is a part: the tyranny of survival. But the harsh reality is that even before we can face the question of survival we must remove layer after layer of "felt needs" (in contrast to "actual needs") that compel us so relentlessly in our consumption. These felt needs, often engendered by commercial forces, stand in the way of an appropriate response to world hunger. "Small is beautiful" (Schumacher)—this recognition is a crucial step in the Church's response to world hunger, for the difficulty is partly technical and partly cultural.

On the domestic level, scarcity of resources has converged with fantastic developments in biomedical technology—especially the capacity to prolong life—to pose most dramatically the question of the distribution and allocation of resources. In the late sixties and early seventies, the difficult question was how to distribute scarce lifesaving medical resources, such as kidney machines and transplants, when it was impossible to provide them to everyone who needed them and qualified for them on medical grounds. Some commentators, such as Joseph Fletcher, argued for selection in terms of utilitarian or social value judgments. Others, including this author, insisted that randomization, a lottery, or queuing would be better mechanisms from a moral standpoint, for they avoid reducing persons to their roles and functions in society, protect equality of opportunity—an analogue of God's indiscriminate care for man—and preserve trust between patient and physician.

Beyond that micro-allocation question are difficult macro-allocation questions. If we think in terms of a budget of time, energy, and money, how much should we allocate to health care and how much to other social goods? Although numerous social goods (such as protecting the environment and eliminating poverty) directly affect health, and other social goods (such as police and fire protection) affect survival, still other social goods (such as art galleries and museums) appeal to values beyond health and survival. After World War II, some German officials decided to rebuild museums and opera houses even before they had enough hospitals. Although health and survival are preconditions for other goods, they should not always take precedence or have priority over those other goods. They are not final, ultimate, or absolute. Quality of life cannot always be subordinated to considerations of quantity of life. Indeed, concentration on the quantity of life has led us to seek its prolongation even when our efforts are pointless and recovery is not a reasonable prospect. We view death as an enemy to be thwarted at all costs.

Second, within the health care budget, how much do we allocate for prevention and how much for rescue or crisis medicine? If, as many medical professionals now think, the environment and one's life-style drastically affect chances of morbidity and premature death, should we concentrate on preventive medicine, particularly since the great investments in life-extending technologies now only produce marginal returns? The matter of personal life-style raises difficult questions. The Church tends to share with liberalism a presumption against interfering with a person's life-style merely to reduce risks for that person—the risk of cigarette smoking, for instance. Of course, one's freedom may legitimately be restricted in order to protect others. To what extent may one's freedom be restricted on paternalistic grounds? Can we prohibit some conduct (such as cigarette smoking) or require certain acts (such as a certain amount of exercise)? And how may we interfere—coercion, inducement, education, explanation of risks? Can society say that an individual who takes certain risks—a cigarette smoker who develops lung cancer—must then bear the cost? All these questions will become increasingly important as we face the fact that crisis intervention has only marginal returns in prolonging life or improving its quality, and is less effective and efficient than preventive medicine.

CONSCIENCE AND PUBLIC ETHICS

A perennial problem for the Christian community is the relation between conscience and the state. Certainly it is a mistake only to state this relation negatively as conscience *versus* or *against* the state, for the relation is more often one of cooperation not conflict. Several of my points concern the way the Christian community can articulate a standard that can guide Christians in their public responsibilities and mesh with general public ethics.

One function of the doctrines of natural law is to offer a basis for cooperation between Christians and non-Christians. Some contend that we need to rehabilitate natural law, which has served to legitimate and limit the political order as well as to guide public policy. Because of various theological and other objections to doctrines of natural law, we may find some other phrase, such as "public ethics," more satisfactory. Policy-makers appeal to standards such as utility, equality, and liberty to justify their policies, and Christians can join in discourse about the meaning and implications of these standards. For instance, what do commitments to liberty and equality indicate about a policy of busing for school desegregation? One should not expect easy answers, for as Max Weber suggested, "Politics is a strong and slow boring of hard boards." And as Reinhold Niebuhr put it, we can only hope for "proximate solutions to insoluble problems."

The Church should also probe the religious and quasi-religious presuppositions of values, principles, and policies, particularly those expressed in the symbols, beliefs, and rituals of the "civil religion." Although we should criticize the Church's easy capitulation to civil religion, we should not compare only the *worst* manifestations of civil religion—its chauvinism, for example—with the *best* manifestations of Christianity. Civil religion, according to Robert Bellah, "has neither been so general that it has lacked incisive relevance to the American scene nor so particular that it has placed American society above universal human values." At its best, it does more than hallow existing institutions and policies, for it embodies symbols—drawn from but now relatively independent of Judaism and Christianity—which can be used to criticize as well as to support institutions and policies.

Although "conscience versus the state" is a distortion, and although the Church should grant the state a presumption of support and obedience, we often face "either/or" conflicts. In such situations, Christian policy-makers may try to protect their integrity by refusing to be agents of injustice. They may resign from public office rather than violate public standards or private convictions. Citizens may refuse to obey some laws on grounds of conscience in an attempt to change those laws by civil disobedience. In some circumstances, the *ultima ratio* of revolutionary force may be warranted.

Jesus insisted, "Render unto Caesar the things that are Caesar's and unto God the things that are God's." (Matt. 22:21) Neither that statement nor Peter's affirmation, "We must obey God rather than men" (Acts 5:29), indicate where the line is to be drawn between loyalty to God and loyalty to Caesar. In each age the Church has to redraw the line according to the nature of the regime. There are, nevertheless, limits which the Church must hold before its members whether they are only citizens or also policy-makers. The Church should grant the state the presumption of support, service, and obedience, but this presumption can never become an absolute obligation. The Christian remains a citizen of two kingdoms with loyalties to both.

The Church is only one community among many, and yet it must never underestimate the power of its witness. While the Church must ultimately bear its witness with integrity and leave the consequences to God, it has a penultimate interest in effectiveness—for instance, in shaping the standards that guide public decisions. A Harris poll in late 1973 discovered that only two of twenty-two institutions drew support from a majority of those questioned. Fifty-seven percent trusted the medical profession, and fifty-two percent had confidence in local trash collectors! The other institutions, including the police, the press, the Congress, the White House, and *religion*, commanded little respect and trust! The Church's effectiveness hinges on its fidelity and integrity.

chapter 22

ONCE AGAIN:
TO COMFORT OR TO CHALLENGE?

Urban T. Holmes III

In January of 1975 the Hartford Appeal was issued. It was prepared under the leadership of two Lutherans, Peter Berger and Richard Neuhaus. In January of 1976 a rejoinder, the Boston Affirmations, was made public. I gather that Max Stackhouse and Constance Parvey were among the principal enablers of this document. While I find myself in considerable agreement with both statements *per se*—perhaps only an indication of my own vapidity and lack of sagacity—one wonders what is the source of the apparent polarity setting apart the two lists of theses.

In some ways the Hartford Appeal and the Boston Affirmations recall a debate raised in a sociological study of the Episcopal Church of the early fifties, published some ten years later, entitled *To Comfort or to Challenge*. Written by several sociologists at the University of California in Berkeley, the question they asked was whether or not the task of the Church is to comfort its members, who are suffering from a loss of self-esteem in the world-at-large, or to challenge its people to right social wrongs. They discovered—to the surprise of very few—that the Church is *de facto* in the comforting business. The authors of this study argue that, while comforting is a valid function, the Church should challenge the social system as well.

The sharpening of the question—to comfort or to challenge—is a post-World War II phenomenon. It is a welcome clarification of a paramount issue brewing in the life of the Church for about a century. Why just a century? Because it is over this period that the Church has become increasingly aware of its own peripheral relationship to the civil order, which has itself evolved over the previous hundred years. It can be said with justification that for fourteen hundred years, until the late eighteenth century, the Church, be it Eastern or Western, Protestant or Catholic, has been in cahoots with the state. This cooperation has taken various forms, all of which have fallen under the category of the so-called Constantinian Church. It was the traumatic events that followed upon the industrial revolution in the West that precipitated the lingering death of the Constantinian Church and has brought the Christian community to ask itself whether the main purpose of the Gospel is to comfort the afflicted or to afflict the comfortable.

There is a certain endemic fear among those generally known as the social activists, those who would choose the second of these two possible agendas, that in fact the Marxian criticism of religion is true. Christianity has been a tool in the hands of the powerful to maintain the status quo by offering a placebo to the oppressed. The language of transcendence, with its emphasis upon a better life after death for those who have been faithful whatever their station in life, sounds to them very much like a use of religion to quell notions of revolution and to keep the masses in subjugation.

The term "social activist" carries for many Church people today a good bit of negative "baggage"—instigation of riots, insensitivity to the ambiguity of motives, disregard for tradition—which is only confirmed for their critics by the acceptance of Marx's criticism of religion. The truth is, however, that the biblical basis of social activism is quite clear. The movement can be seen as a reemergence of the Old Testament prophetic tradition, which confronts the injustice of the world in the name of the Lord. We are reminded of Nathan, Elijah, Amos, Micah, the first Isaiah, and Jeremiah. With its roots in the Christian Socialist Movement—of which the eminent Anglican theologian, F.D. Maurice, was a member—social activism has shown itself in this country in three "waves": the optimism of the Social Gospel, the chastened pessimism of Reinhold Niebuhr and his school, and the more contemporary liberation theology. Each of these movements has, in its own way, called upon the Church to see the locus of the Gospel in the confrontation of the injustice of the world in the name of Christ. The Boston Affirmations stand squarely in this traditoin.

Social activism arose out of the disruption of society, the disenchantment of western culture, and the disestablishment of the Church. The industrial revolution and rapid urbanization undermined the internal cohesion of an essentially agrarian society. The eighteenth-century Enlightenment, followed by post-Kantian philosophy and the rise of the human sciences—psychology, sociology, political sciences, economics—was both a stimulus to and an expression of a developing secularism. The demise of the acknowledged civil role of the Church was almost the inevitable result. Social activism as a response to this progression of events—disruption, disenchantment, and disestablishment—possesses both strength and weakness.

There is little doubt that to the extent that the Gospel has been encapsulated within the expectations of that state and its established Church, serving to legitimate the all-too-human system, the radical judgment of God on our pretensions has been obscured and the freedom given in Christ rendered impotent. The demise of the Constantinian Church has liberated the Gospel, while it has threatened many "respectable Christians." There is no question whatsoever that he who separates his private from his public life, and at best confines his religious faith to a comforting of the former, deserves to be far more than just threatened. Herein lies the strength of social activism.

The weakness of social activism is its easy identification with the secular culture and all its "catch phrases." The irony is that while the death of the Constantinian Church liberated the *prophetic* witness of the Gospel over aginst the world, it rendered the worldview (the cognitive filters) of many churchmen vulnerable to the seductions of secularism. The spokesmen for the Boston Affirmations believe themselves to be biblical and patristic (ante-Nicene) in outlook, working out of a notion of "salvation history" and a theology of hope. This may be implicitly the case, but there is an explicit tone of secularism against which the Hartford Appeal speaks. *Simplistic* statements about a perfect society, the unqualified condemnation of human institutions, the adulation of human potential, and the enthusiastic pursuit of programs and planning—all of which are questioned in the Hartford Appeal—easily adopt the coloring, if not the conviction, of those who put all their hope in this present age.

The authors of the Boston Affirmations, if I am correctly informed, believe that the Hartford Appeal is "wrong-headed" and gives comfort to those who would flee the stark reality of an unjust world. It tends toward a gnostic dualism, which is more negative than positive, and it gives permission for persons to hide behind testimonies to the transcendence of God and life beyond the grave. The social activists have a reason to be apprehensive. There has been an unquestioned withdrawal in the Church from confrontation, sometimes by those very persons who were leading marches in the sixties. We are in the midst of a wave of pietism (the neo-Pentecostals, Faith Alive, the Cursillo movement), with its emphasis upon the emotional experience of God, inner reflection supported by small groups, and a kind of popular dualism of nature and supernature. The pietist tells us that what is wrong with the world is the corruption of the individual heart, perhaps adding that it results in the contamination of the material world. The solution is to "accept the Lord Jesus in your heart." This is obviously simplistic to a frightening degree.

If the reader will notice, I have described the *perceived* (as by their opponents) supporters of the Boston Affirmations and the Hartford Appeal as both simplistic. Despite protestations to the contrary by their proponents, the authors of the Hartford Appeal are obviously skeptical about the commitment of the social activists, as represented in the Boston Affirmations, to the God revealed in Christ. My guess is that they see them still in the context of radical ("death of God") theology, which had more Madison Avenue promotion than theological substance. In turn, the signers of the Boston Affirmations cannot help but see the authors of the Hartford Appeal as a bunch of scalawags and carpetbaggers, trading on the decline of prophecy and the rise of piety. What each group is saying to the other, from their own perspective, is that the fullness of the Gospel is much more than the opposition is perceived to be making it.

This is certainly true. The Gospel is always more than anyone makes it, but particularly when we are pressing for our program. It is my conviction that polemic serves the Church, but only to a point. That point is when we have to make a choice of one position over against the other. I believe in a dialectical theology. I am confident that heresy, which comes from a Greek word meaning "to choose," arises when we close our minds to the polemics of the opposition and stand our ground; because God's "ground" is always infinitely larger than ours. Orthodoxy, which means literally "straight thinking," is served only when we are willing to hold in our mind seeming opposites. Examples of such opposites are: that Jesus Christ is fully man and fully God in one person, and that God is three persons in one nature. Carl Jung, the father of analytical psychology, argued in his *Answer to Job* (Princeton: Princeton University Press, 1972) that the very nature of God is paradoxical. Whether that be true or not, it does appear that the telling of parables, of which Jesus was so fond, is a literary form that challenges the certainties of the faithful by the juxtaposition of opposites.

Behind my argument for orthodoxy as dialectical is my belief that man is finite. It is only in the infinite mind of God that we can hope for a resolution of the conflict of apparent opposites. When we draw to a premature resolution of this tension, it is a clear indication that the sin of man has triumphed over openness to the word of God. If I were to say, for example, *either* that the Gospel means that man is in himself self-authenticated *or* that the injustice of capitalism or communism is no concern of the Gospel, I will have succumbed in a telling way to the seductions of evil.

My hope for the Episcopal Church is that it will take seriously a dialectical theology. This needs to be explained, but first two matters demand our brief attention. I am not sure the Episcopal Church as a whole understands the urgency of the question that confronts the post-Constantinian Church: Has the Gospel anything to say to late twentieth-century man? If it does, the Episcopal Church seems to shrink from the hard work of an answer.

First, the Episcopal Church has to acknowledge that over the last two hundred years we have gone through a period of disruption, disenchantment, and disestablishment. We have trouble believing this. I have been asked within the year by sincere Church people how I can possibly suggest we do not live in a Christian society, I know priests who still think we can do business as if we were seventeenth-century English parsons, and I see those who wish to cling to ecclesiastical privilege and cannot understand the debilitating effect of a patronizing anticlericalism prevalent in the land. It is easy to get the impression that the Church went to sleep in 1750 and, like Rip Van Winkle, is perpetually reawakening to its own confusion.

Second, the Episcopal Church must realize that all problems are theological problems, and anti-intellectualism is demonic seducation. We hide our anti-intellectualism under the cult of the common man, with appeals to "popular" theology and attacks on the esoteric interests of theologians. (The word "esoteric" means "inner" or "interior"—in other words, gnostic. I personally find some things in the pietistic movement far more given to an inner gnosticism than most theology.) Undoubtedly there are theologians who revel in their jargon or enjoy being obscure. Yet the above is no reason to flee the need for thinking. Theology is *thinking about religion*, and thinking requires a certain discipline and at least a modicum of tools, such as a vocabulary. Theology is the only means to obtain distance on our experience and its issues and to avoid *ad hominem* solutions (those based on emotion or unexamined common sense). While we do need to abrogate theology for its own sake, it is theology—good or bad—that makes the difference. If theology is difficult, then let's train ourselves.

Having introduced these two provisos, what is it that a dialectical theology, in the area of concerns found in the Hartford Appeal and the Boston Affirmations, requires of the Episcopal Church in the next ten years? One thing which lies behind the Boston Affirmations, stated more or less in passing, is the belief that the human sciences must be taken seriously as providing the data for a Christian understanding of man. The tripartite doctrine of man—spirit, soul, and body—which dominated Christian anthropology from the second to the nineteenth centuries, was derived from the psychology of Middle Platonism (a second-century eclectical philosophy drawing on Platonism, Stoicism, and Pythagoreanism). A tripartite anthropology allows us to think of man as principally a disembodied "spirit" or "soul." It lies behind the notion that the "real concern" of the Gospel is the salvation of souls irrespective of the injustice of this world. It encourages a kind of idealism that ignores feelings. A tripartite anthropology has no more authority than its ability to illuminate our experience, and certainly most of us would hold that contemporary psychology, sociology, and anthropology do a better job of that.

A contemporary Christian understanding of man holds that man does not *have* a body, a community, and a history; man *is* his body, community, and history. If we are to speak of human "nature" or the being (ontology) of man, it must include his physical makeup, his social world, and his past. The goal of salvation is the wholeness of man ("hominisation" is the theological term), which means a wholeness in terms of body, community, and history. Sexuality becomes an issue in the doctrine of salvation. Freedom in Christ is not possible unless a person lives in a community in which such freedom is possible. The healing of our memories is vital to our redemption. One does not divide the world into two realms, the sacred and profane; there is, rather, a sacred center within the total world which defines the goal of all human understanding and will not let us call any truth "unclean."

The time is long past when the Episcopal Church can allow itself the luxury of that stupidity of dismissing unpleasant truth as "sociology" or "psychology." Obviously, reductions of human nature to one or more of the social sciences is something to be abhorred, as is all scientism; but we can ill afford to ignore the depths of human meaning that the appropriate use of such disciplines opens to the theologian and the average churchgoer. Contemporary learning is not opposed, as some suggest, to biblical insights. To use the latter to avoid the challenge of the former is to ignore the Holy Spirit speaking through tradition and reason, as any good Anglican believes he does. Tradition is a living thing, on which each age puts its mark. It is not to be received and handed on as some inviolable package. Our times may not, as the Hartford Appeal suggests, be in possession of a definitive word, but certainly they have a potential for true insight as legitimate as the fourth, thirteenth, or sixteenth centuries.

If we believe this, as I think we should, the Church cannot at the same time lose the vision of a transcendent God who creates, redeems, and sanctifies his world by being present and known within it and yet is infinitely more than this world. This belief in transcendence lies at the very heart of the Christian worldview. We can never settle for secularism or pantheism as a philosophy. While we believe that God created man with reason, and consequently is responsible for himself as embodied within a community and living out his history, we always insist that he work out his salvation under the vision of eternity. We become fully human by grace through faith.

I sometimes hear it said that the "old spirituality" no longer works. I am never quite sure what the "old spirituality" is. If we mean by this attendance at the daily office twice a day, family prayers lasting thirty minutes, and fish on Friday, I can probably agree. If we mean, on the other hand, taking seriously the openness of man to a redemptive relationship with a personal transcendent God, fed by the divine presence in the world now and appropriated through a disciplined life, then I cannot agree. The mobility and fast pace of our life may call into question certain spiritual "programs," but it does not abolish the Christian perception of the relationship between God and man in whatever period of history we find ourselves. I find myself very much at one with the Hartford Appeal at this point.

A dialectical theology would not allow a spiritual life to lapse into pietism any more than it would permit a concern for justice and human rights to become a mere secular program. The absence of a dialectical theology has done both these things. We have been asked to choose whether we are interested in prayer or social action, transcendence or immanence, tradition or relevance, orthodoxy or ethicalism, content or process, the Bible or psychology. It is time for the Episcopal Church to refuse to make any such choice and to live with the apparent contradictions embodied in the acceptance of mutually exclusive categories.

When I was in graduate school I remember one of my professors, after a particularly hard day in class, saying, "I am so tired of arguing about transcendence and immanence." Perhaps many of us are, but the issue is with us for the duration. It is certainly true that Christianity is a revealed religion, which means that the knowledge of God is not something we have derived from our examination of life, but is a gift of God's self-disclosure in history. If that is true, we cannot escape the issue of transcendence and immanence, but have to live in the seeming contradiction that a God who is other than we and our world (transcendence) makes himself known in this present age (immanence). This is not just a matter of the content of belief, but it also has to do with our action. For the knowledge that is given in revelation from above reveals to us God's purpose for a broken and incomplete world and demands of us that we become his instruments of justice and love here below.

The world is not divided into mystics and prophets. A true mystic cannot help but act and a true prophet is a mystic in action. It has been popular in the last generation or so in the Old Testament studies to oppose to one another the priests (members of the Hartford Appeal?) and the prophets (signers of the Boston Affirmations?) of Israel and Judah. This is a very superficial reading of the Scriptures. There is no question but that there is a tension in the image of some who serve in the Temple waiting upon the Lord, and some who stand in the marketplace denouncing the oppression of the poor. The tension is necessary to the Church and to every churchman; to know that God loves and comforts us and to know that he is angry and challenges our sin.

Love is not mere sentimentality, with no price and a call to an easy reconciliation. Prophecy is not just another program of community organization and confrontation with no sense of a God known in the sacraments and in prayer. A total faith demands an expression in a dialectical theology, which gives meaning to every facet of our life and directs it with a purity or singleness of heart or mind to the vision of God for his creation. We cannot choose to pray or to march, we have to do both if we take the Gospel seriously. This the Episcopal Church must understand if it is not to be seduced by every swing of the pendulum and left impotent before the Lord.

contributors

George D. Browne, Bishop of Liberia, is a graduate of Cuttington College and Virginia Theological Seminary. He has served various parishes in Liberia and was Chaplain of Cuttington College from 1968–1970.

Edmond L. Browning was elected Bishop of Hawaii on May 1, 1976. He has been Executive for National and World mission of the Episcopal Church, Bishop of Okinawa, Japan (1968–1971) and Bishop-in-Charge of the Convocation of American Churches in Europe (1971–1974).

Marllene Campbell is a Dakota Indian and the wife of a priest of the Episcopal Church.

James M. Childress is Joseph P. Kennedy, Sr. Professor of Christian Ethics at the Center for Bioethics, Kennedy Institute, Georgetown University, Washington, D.C. Formerly Professor of Ethics at the University of Virginia, he is the author of *Civil Disobedience and Political Obligation* and *Secularization and the Protestant Prospect*.

Anthony Damron, O.S.B. is Prior of St. Gregory's Abbey, Three Rivers, Michigan. He is the author of a variety of articles concerning religious orders.

Philip Deemer is the past editor of *New Life*, a journal devoted to the renewal of the Church. He is now President of the Anchor Society, located in San Francisco, California.

O. C. Edwards, Jr. is Dean of Seabury-Western Theological Seminary. He is a noted New Testament scholar, distinguished preacher, and the author of numerous articles and books, including *How It All Began* and *The Living and Active Word*.

Norman J. Faramelli is Co-Director of the Boston Industrial Mission with which he has been associated for many years.

Urban T. Holmes III is the Dean of the School of Theology at the University of the South. His field of special interest is theology and culture, and he is the author of a number of books and articles, including *The Future Shape of Ministry* and *Ministry and Imagination*.

Jean Henkel Johnson is a representative from the Episcopal Church to the National Anglican/Roman Catholic Consultation. Wife of the former Dean of the Church Divinity School of the Pacific, Mrs. Johnson has long been active in Episcopal Church work and ministry.

John M. Krumm is the Bishop of Southern Ohio. He is a member of the Joint Commission on Ecumenical Relations and a representative of the Episcopal Church to the Conference on Christian Unity (COCU).

Dolores R. Leckey is a Roman Catholic layperson, who is very active in Church renewal in the Washington area. She serves as a consultant to the Metropolitan Ecumenical Training Center and Inter-Met in the area of spirituality.

Clifton K. Meador, a physician, is Chief of Medicine, St. Thomas' Hospital, Nashville, Tennessee, and an active Episcopalian.

Paul Moore, Jr. is Bishop of New York and former Suffragan Bishop of Washington, D.C. He has been involved in urban ministry in Jersey City, New Jersey (1949–1957) and was Dean and Rector of Christ Church Cathedral, Indianapolis from 1957–1963.

William C. Spong is Professor of Pastoral Theology at the Episcopal Theological Seminary of the Southwest, Austin, Texas. He is also an accredited supervisor of the Association for Clinical Pastoral Education and previously was chaplain at Duke University Hospital, Durham, North Carolina.

Furman C. Stough is Bishop of Alabama. A graduate of the University of the South and St. Luke's School of Theology, Bishop Stough has been Rector of Great Sheffield, Alabama; All Souls, Machinato, Okinawa; and St. John's, Decatur, Illinois.

John H. Westerhoff III is Associate Professor of Religion and Education at Duke University, Durham, North Carolina. He was founding editor of *Colloquy,* a journal devoted to Christian education, is a well known speaker and author of numerous books, including *Values for Tomorrow's Children* and *Will Our Children Have Faith?*

Roger J. White is Rector of St. Paul's Church, Alton, Illinois. A native of Leeds, England, he is a graduate of Kelham Theological College and Eden Theological Seminary.

Louis J. Willie is Executive Vice-President of the Booker T. Washington Insurance Company and Vice-President and Secretary-Treasurer of Citizens Federal Savings and Loan Association, Birmingham, Alabama. A member of St. Mark's Church, Birmingham, he has been active in Church and community affairs for many years.

Charles L. Winters is Professor of Dogmatic Theology at the School of Theology of the University of the South. Dr. Winters is also Director of the program of Theological Education by Extension.

John W. Yates II is Assistant, St. Stephen's Church, Sewickley, Pennsylvania.

Arthur E. Zannoni is an Old Testament scholar and active Roman Catholic layman. Having served a year on the faculty of the School of Theology of the University of the South as a sabbatical replacement, he is now on the faculty of the University of Notre Dame, teaching in an extension program in West Lafayette, Indiana.

bibliography

Allen, Roland, *Missionary Methods: St. Paul's Or Ours* (Grand Rapids, Mich.: Wm. B. Eerdmans Co., 1962).
A basic work on a non-stipendary priesthood and a new look at Church strategy in small communities.

Anderson, Gerald H. and Thomas F. Stransky, eds., *Mission Trends No. 1* (New York: Paulist Press, 1974).
Twenty-three chapters from world-wide Church leaders that discuss crucial mission topics, including the missionary message and goals, the missionary, Churches in mission, liberation and humanization.

Anderson, Gerald H. and Thomas F. Stransky, eds., *Mission Trends No. 2: Evangelization* (New York: Paulist Press, 1975).
Twenty-two important essays discuss the meaning and mandate of evangelization, priorities and strategies, other faiths and evangelization, pluralism and proselytism. Five important Roman Catholic, Orthodox, and Protestant evangelism statements are included in an appendix.

Berger, Peter L. and Richard John Neuhaus, *Against the World for the World* (New York: The Seabury Press, 1976).
Contains the Hartford Appeal statement and a collection of interpretative chapters which discuss its meaning and implications for religion and theology.

Carr, Oscar C., ed., *Jesus, Dollars and Sense* (New York: The Seabury Press, 1976).
A practical guidebook on stewardship in the churches.

Green, Michael, *Evangelism in the Early Church* (Grand Rapids, Mich: Wm. B. Eerdmans Co., 1970).
A comprehensive, historical examination of evangelism.

Gustafson, James M. and James T. Laney, ed., *On Being Responsible* (New York: Harper and Row, 1968).
A basic, very useful reader on contemporary problems and topics of Christian ethics.

Herzog, Frederick, *Liberation Theology* (New York: The Seabury Press, 1972).
One of the introductory examinations and discussions of liberation thought.

Holmes, Urban T. III, *Young Children and the Eucharist* (New York: The Seabury Press, 1972).
A comprehensive discussion of the Eucharist and education in the Church.

Howe, Reuel L., *Man's Need and God's Action* (New York: The Seabury Press, 1953).

Still one of the best introductions and guides to the Church's mission and Christian faith exploration.

Kübler-Ross, Elisabeth, *Questions and Answers on Death and Dying* (New York: Macmillan, 1974).

A basic, very popular work on pastoral care of the dying.

Merton, Thomas, *Contemplative Prayer* (New York: Doubleday, 1971).

A basic, readable introduction to contemplative prayer by one of the great mystics of the twentieth century.

Neill, Stephen, *Anglicanism* (Baltimore: Penguin Books, 1958).

A highly readable, interesting, and extremely competent guide to the history, traditions, and thought of Anglicanism.

Neill, Stephen, *History of Christian Missions* (Baltimore: Penguin Books, 1964).

A readable and comprehensive history that is especially well organized and easy to understand.

Niebuhr, Reinhold, *An Interpretation of Christian Ethics* (New York: Meridian Books, 1956).

A basic introduction and guide to Christian ethics. Although this is an older book, it remains one of the best beginning books on the subject.

Nouwen, Henri J. M., *Reaching Out* (New York: Doubleday, 1975).

This book is an example of a new kind of spirituality that is closely related to pastoral care.

Ramsey, Paul, *The Patient as Person* (New Haven: Yale University Press, 1970).

One of the most complete basic introductions to medical ethics.

Westerhoff, John H. III, *Values for Tomorrow's Children* (Philadelphia: Pilgrim Press, 1970).

A refreshing and lively reconsideration of values and education in the Church.

Westerhoff, John H. III, *Will Our Children Have Faith?* (New York: The Seabury Press, 1976).

A reconsideration of religious education and its mission in the Church. An especially important book by a leading Christian educator.

Winter, Gibson, *New Creation as Metroplis* (New York: Macmillan, 1965).

A classic discussion of urban mission and affairs with a theological perspective.